HOPE
for TODAY

HOPE
for TODAY

JOHN'S ACCOUNT
of the LIFE *of* JESUS

GOD'S WORD® Translation

BakerBooks
a division of Baker Publishing Group
Grand Rapids, Michigan

Contents

1

Hope for a Troubled World

The purpose of God's saving, life-changing message—so plainly revealed in John's account of Jesus' ministry—is clear: "These miracles have been written so that you will believe that Jesus is the Messiah, the Son of God, and so that you will have life by believing in him" (John 20:31).

Believing this *really* Good News provides you with *real* hope in this troubled and complex world. As Jesus said, "I've told you this so that my peace will be with you. In the world you'll have trouble. But cheer up! I have overcome the world" (John 16:33).

The world, of course, attempts to establish peace by eliminating the external problems that cause distress and anxiety. Jesus Christ promises, however, to provide internal peace to everyone who believes in him in spite of the external problems that trouble them. By trusting in him—even though you may be surrounded by trouble and uncertainty—you can have real hope and real peace of mind!

John's account in the New Testament of the Bible is only a small part of God's revelation to us. One of the particular beauties of John's writing is that it clearly illustrates God's plan to save us and answers some of the most common questions about Jesus.

Trust in Jesus Christ and his promise: "I'm leaving you peace. I'm giving you my peace. I don't give you the kind of peace that the world gives. So don't be troubled" (John 14:27).

That's *really* Good News!

2

Knowing What God Thinks about You

If you're like most people, you're very concerned about what other people think of you. You hope that others think of you as successful, thoughtful, attractive, and so on. You hope that people like you.

However, you should be far more concerned about what God thinks about you. So, take a few moments and ask yourself the following important questions: What does God think about me? How can I be certain?

What Does God Think about You?

The following concepts based on God's revelation—as recorded in the Bible—will help you understand what God thinks about you and other humans.

Originally, humans were created good.

Then God said, "Let us make humans in our image, in our likeness . . ." So God created humans in his image . . . He created them male and female. And God saw everything that he had made and that it was very good.

Genesis 1:26–27, 31

Then sin spoiled everything! As a result, our natural human condition wasn't good anymore—it became corrupted. In other words, we all have a problem.

The world was corrupt in God's sight and full of violence.

Genesis 6:11

The Lord saw how evil humans had become on the earth. All day long their deepest thoughts were nothing but evil.

Genesis 6:5

Indeed, I was born guilty.
I was a sinner when my mother conceived me.

Psalm 51:5

Not one person has God's approval.
No one has understanding.
No one searches for God.
Everyone has turned away.
Together they have become rotten to the
core.
No one does anything good,
not even one person.

Romans 3:10–12

The consequences of this problem—our corrupted human condition—are not good!

> We did what our corrupt desires and thoughts wanted us to do. So, because of our nature, we deserved God's anger just like everyone else.
>
> Ephesians 2:3

> As a result, people have no excuse. They knew God but did not praise and thank him for being God. Instead, their thoughts were pointless, and their misguided minds were plunged into darkness. While claiming to be wise, they became fools. They exchanged the glory of the immortal God for statues that looked like humans, birds, animals, and snakes. . . .
>
> And because they thought it was worthless to acknowledge God, God allowed their own immoral minds to control them. So they do these indecent things. Their lives are filled with all kinds of sexual sins, wickedness, and greed. They are mean. They are filled with envy, murder, quarreling, deceit, and viciousness. They are gossips, slanderers, haters of God, haughty, arrogant, and boastful. They think up new ways to be cruel. They don't obey their parents, don't have any sense, don't keep promises, and don't show love to their own families or mercy to others. Although they know God's judgment that those who do such things deserve to die, they not only do these things but also approve of others who do them.
>
> Romans 1:20–23, 28–32

This is a real problem, because as sinners we're separated from God. As sinners we are condemned by God.

> But your wrongs have separated you from your
> God,
> > and your sins have made him hide his face
> > so that he doesn't hear you.

Isaiah 59:2

> The payment for sin is death.

Romans 6:23

Remember, although God created us in his image, sin spoiled everything. As a result, we aren't perfect anymore. "Because all people have sinned, they have fallen short of God's glory (Romans 3:23). But God wants us to be perfect. In fact, he requires us to be perfect like him.

> Be holy because I, the LORD your God, am holy.

Leviticus 19:2

However, if you admit that you have sinned, "God is faithful and reliable. If we confess our sins, he forgives them and cleanses us from everything we've done wrong" (1 John 1:9). And if you believe that Jesus Christ died for you—as your substitute and Savior—on the cross, you are not condemned by God.

> God sent his Son into the world, not to condemn the world, but to save the world. Those who believe in him won't be condemned.

John 3:17–18

So those who are believers in Christ Jesus can no longer be condemned.

Romans 8:1

Once you were separated from God. . . . But now Christ has brought you back to God by dying in his physical body. He did this so that you could come into God's presence without sin, fault, or blame.

Colossians 1:21–22

The payment for sin is death, but the gift that God freely gives is everlasting life found in Christ Jesus our Lord.

Romans 6:23

God had Christ, who was sinless, take our sin so that we might receive God's approval through him.

2 Corinthians 5:21

In other words, Jesus has taken care of the problem!

We were dead because of our failures, but he made us alive together with Christ. (It is God's kindness that saved you.) God has brought us back to life together with Christ Jesus and has given us a position in heaven with him. He did this through Christ Jesus out of his generosity to us in order to show his extremely rich kindness in the world to come. God saved you through faith as an act of kindness. You had nothing to do with it. Being saved is a gift from God. It's not the result of anything you've done, so no one can brag about it.

Ephesians 2:5–9

But now through Christ Jesus you, who were once far away, have been brought near by the blood of Christ.

Ephesians 2:13

Indeed, we, too, were once stupid, disobedient, and misled. We were slaves to many kinds of lusts and pleasures. We were mean and jealous. We were hated, and we hated each other. However, when God our Savior made his kindness and love for humanity appear, he saved us, but not because of anything we had done to gain his approval. Instead, because of his mercy he saved us through the washing in which the Holy Spirit gives us new birth and renewal. God poured a generous amount of the Spirit on us through Jesus Christ our Savior. As a result, God in his kindness has given us his approval and we have become heirs who have the confidence that we have everlasting life.

Titus 3:3–7

Your Relationship with God

Believing that Jesus Christ died for you completely changes your relationship with God. In fact, by believing in Jesus you become a new person, with the power to overcome sin and live a life that pleases the one true God.

Whoever is a believer in Christ is a new creation. The old way of living has disappeared. A new way of living has come into existence. God has done all this. He has restored our relationship with him through Christ. . . . In other words, God was using Christ to restore his relationship with humanity. He didn't hold people's faults against them, and he has given us this message of restored relationships to tell others. Therefore, we are Christ's representatives, and through us God is calling you. We beg you on behalf of Christ to become reunited with God. God had Christ, who was sinless, take our sin so that we might receive God's approval through him.

2 Corinthians 5:17–21

You were also taught to become a new person created to be like God, truly righteous and holy.

Ephesians 4:24

Imitate God, since you are the children he loves. Live in love as Christ also loved us. He gave his life for us as an offering and sacrifice.... Determine which things please the Lord. Have nothing to do with the useless works that darkness produces.

Ephesians 5:1–2, 10–11

How Can You Be Certain?

God says he loves you. But how can you be certain that an unseen God really loves you? The following passages from the Bible—God's inspired Word—reveal God's unconditional love for you.

God loved the world this way: He gave his only Son so that everyone who believes in him will not die but will have eternal life.

John 3:16

Look at it this way: At the right time, while we were still helpless, Christ died for ungodly people. Finding someone who would die for a godly person is rare. (Maybe someone would have the courage to die for a good person.) Christ died for us while we were still sinners. This demonstrates God's love for us.

Romans 5:6–8

God didn't spare his own Son but handed him over to death for all of us. So he will also give us everything along with him.

Romans 8:32

Now You Know

Now you know what God thinks about you!

I'm not ashamed of the Good News. It is God's power to save everyone who believes, Jews first and Greeks as well. God's approval is revealed in this Good News. This approval begins and ends with faith as Scripture says, "The person who has God's approval will live by faith."

Romans 1:16–17

You heard and believed the message of truth, the Good News that he [Christ] has saved you.

Ephesians 1:13

These verses represent only a few of the passages in the Bible that tell you what God thinks about you and how you can be certain. Take a few moments right now to thank God for revealing to you what he thinks about you. Thank him for proving how much he loves you by sending his only Son, Jesus, to die for you.

In fact, you can thank God for giving you *real hope*—now and forever—by praying:

Heavenly Father, I believe, but help my weak faith. Help my faith to grow stronger so that I can be certain that you love me.

Thank you for revealing to me that your Son, Jesus, is my Savior. Thank you for demonstrating how much you love me by sending Jesus to die for me—for my sins and failures—on the cross. Thank you for telling me that I am no longer separated from you and condemned. Now I can be certain that whenever I die I will live with you forever in heaven.

Help me—through the power of the Holy Spirit—to overcome my sins and failures. Help me to change the way I think and act and live a new life that pleases you. Help me to seek your will for my life. Help me to serve others so that other people come to know Jesus as their Savior and Lord through me.

This prayer is offered in the name of your Son, Jesus—my Savior—the One who gives me real hope and makes me certain. Amen!

3

John's Account of the Life of Jesus

The Word Becomes Human

1 ¹In the beginning the Word already existed. The Word was with God, and the Word was God. ²He was already with God in the beginning.

³Everything came into existence through him. Not one thing that exists was made without him.

⁴He was the source of life, and that life was the light for humanity.

⁵The light shines in the dark, and the dark has never extinguished it.

⁶God sent a man named John to be his messenger. ⁷John came to declare the truth about the light so that everyone would become believers through his message. ⁸John was not the light, but he came to declare the truth about the light.

Jesus

Where was Jesus before he was born in Bethlehem? What did he do before he came down to earth? The apostle John clues us in to Jesus' whereabouts in the first chapter of his account of Jesus' ministry. John explains that Jesus was with God in the beginning of time. John calls Jesus "the Word," and he says that "the Word was God." He goes on to explain how Jesus was intimately involved with the whole creation of the world.

⁹The real light, which shines on everyone, was coming into the world. ¹⁰He was in the world, and the world came into existence through him. Yet, the world didn't recognize him. ¹¹He went to his own people, and his own people didn't accept him. ¹²However, he gave the right to become God's children to everyone who believed in him. ¹³These people didn't become God's children in a physical way—from a human impulse or from a husband's desire to have a child. They were born from God.

Faith

The Bible says that faith is a sinful person's acceptance of Jesus as his or her real and only Savior. Such acceptance includes complete reliance on Jesus' perfect life and sacrificial death for the forgiveness of sins and salvation. The Bible also reveals that this faith is not the result of anything a person does, but a work of the Holy Spirit. The person who endures in this faith to the end will have eternal life. Tragically, without such faith no salvation is possible (see also Matthew 24:13; John 3:36; Acts 10:43; 16:31; 1 Corinthians 12:3; Galatians 2:16; 1 Peter 1:5).

¹⁴The Word became human and lived among us. We saw his glory. It was the glory that the Father shares with his only Son, a glory full of kindness and truth.
¹⁵(John declared the truth about him when he said loudly, "This is the person about whom

I said, 'The one who comes after me was before me because he existed before I did.'")

¹⁶Each of us has received one gift after another because of all that the Word is. ¹⁷The Teachings were given through Moses, but kindness and truth came into existence through Jesus Christ. ¹⁸No one has ever seen God. God's only Son, the one who is closest to the Father's heart, has made him known.

John Prepares the Way
(Matthew 3:1–12; Mark 1:1–8; Luke 3:1–18)

¹⁹This was John's answer when the Jews sent priests and Levites from Jerusalem to ask him, "Who are you?" ²⁰John didn't refuse to answer. He told them clearly, "I'm not the Messiah."

²¹They asked him, "Well, are you Elijah?"

John answered, "No, I'm not."

Then they asked, "Are you the prophet?"

John replied, "No."

²²So they asked him, "Who are you? Tell us so that we can take an answer back to those who sent us. What do you say about yourself?"

²³John said, "I'm a voice crying out in the desert, 'Make the way for the Lord straight,' as the prophet Isaiah said."

²⁴Some of those who had been sent were Pharisees. ²⁵They asked John, "Why do you baptize if you're not the Messiah or Elijah or the prophet?"

²⁶John answered them, "I baptize with water. Someone you don't know is standing among you.

²⁷He's the one who comes after me. I am not worthy to untie his sandal strap."

²⁸This happened in Bethany on the east side of the Jordan River, where John was baptizing.

John Identifies Jesus as the Lamb of God

²⁹John saw Jesus coming toward him the next day and said, "Look! This is the Lamb of God who takes away the sin of the world. ³⁰He is the one I spoke about when I said, 'A man who comes after me was before me because he existed before I did.' ³¹I didn't know who he was. However, I came to baptize with water to show him to the people of Israel."

Receiving God's Approval

The Bible says that everything needed to restore our relationship with God was done when Jesus gave his life on the cross. Because of Jesus' sacrificial death, God declared everyone free from the debt and guilt of sin. This freedom becomes the property of an individual through personal acceptance of God's declaration of forgiveness. In other words, all who by faith apply to themselves God's declaration of forgiveness can be confident that they have God's approval—not by any merit of their own, but solely for Christ's sake (see also Acts 10:43; Romans 3:22–24, 28; 5:18–19; 2 Corinthians 5:19; Ephesians 2:8).

The Law in Moses' Teachings

The Bible teaches that the law in Moses' teachings demands perfection of thought, word, and deed; it completely condemns everyone who breaks it. The law in Moses' teachings cannot save sinful people. Its chief function, since Adam and Eve's fall into sin, is to lead humans to the knowledge of their corrupt condition (see also Leviticus 19:2; Deuteronomy 27:26; Matthew 5:48; Romans 3:20).

The Human Condition

The Bible reveals that humans were made by God through an act of direct creation, given an immortal soul, endowed with a perfect nature, and created to live forever with God. However, our first parents, Adam and Eve, sinned and broke their relationship with God. As a result, their human nature was corrupted and they became subject to death. In our corrupt nature we cannot, by any powers of our own, restore our relationship with God (see also Genesis 1:27; 2:7; 3; Psalms 14:3; 143:2; Isaiah 64:6; Romans 5:12; 1 Corinthians 2:14).

Despite these clear statements in the Bible, many people still ask, "But I'm a good person! Isn't that enough to get into heaven?"

Once again, the Bible details the dilemma of the human condition. The most widely recognized laws in Moses' teachings are the Ten Commandments:

> Never have any other god. Never make your own carved idols or statues that represent any creature in the sky, on the earth, or in the water. Never worship them or serve them, because I, the Lord your God, am a God who does not tolerate rivals . . .
> Never use the name of the Lord your God carelessly.
> Remember the day of worship by observing it as a holy day.
> Honor your father and your mother, so that you may live for a long time in the land the Lord your God is giving you.
> Never murder.
> Never commit adultery.
> Never steal.
> Never lie when you testify about your neighbor.
> Never desire to take your neighbor's household away from him.
> Never desire to take your neighbor's wife, his male or female slave, his ox, his donkey, or anything else that belongs to him.
>
> Exodus 20:1–17

We all have violated one or more of these commandments at one time or another in our lives. The dilemma for us occurs when we realize how God looks at sin—the failure to keep his commandments perfectly!

If we follow all these commandments all our lives but break just one, one time, we disqualify ourselves for God's kingdom. The only remedy is trusting totally in Jesus!

³²John said, "I saw the Spirit come down as a dove from heaven and stay on him. ³³I didn't know who he was. But God, who sent me to baptize with

water, had told me, 'When you see the Spirit come down and stay on someone, you'll know that person is the one who baptizes with the Holy Spirit.' ³⁴I have seen this and have declared that this is the Son of God."

Calling of the First Disciples

³⁵The next day John was standing with two of his disciples. ³⁶John saw Jesus walk by. John said, "Look! This is the Lamb of God." ³⁷When the two disciples heard John say this, they followed Jesus.

³⁸Jesus turned around and saw them following him. He asked them, "What are you looking for?"

They said to him, "Rabbi" (which means "teacher"), "where are you staying?"

³⁹Jesus told them, "Come, and you will see." So they went to see where he was staying and spent the rest of that day with him. It was about ten o'clock in the morning.

⁴⁰Andrew, Simon Peter's brother, was one of the two disciples who heard John and followed Jesus. ⁴¹Andrew at once found his brother Simon and told him, "We have found the Messiah" (which means "Christ"). ⁴²Andrew brought Simon to Jesus.

Jesus looked at Simon and said, "You are Simon, son of John. Your name will be Cephas" (which means "Peter").

⁴³The next day Jesus wanted to go to Galilee. He found Philip and told him, "Follow me!" ⁴⁴(Philip

was from Bethsaida, the hometown of Andrew and Peter.)

⁴⁵Philip found Nathanael and told him, "We have found the man whom Moses wrote about in his teachings and whom the prophets wrote about. He is Jesus, son of Joseph, from the city of Nazareth."

⁴⁶Nathanael said to Philip, "Can anything good come from Nazareth?"

Philip told him, "Come and see!"

⁴⁷Jesus saw Nathanael coming toward him and remarked, "Here is a true Israelite who is sincere."

⁴⁸Nathanael asked Jesus, "How do you know anything about me?"

Jesus answered him, "I saw you under the fig tree before Philip called you."

⁴⁹Nathanael said to Jesus, "Rabbi, you are the Son of God! You are the king of Israel!"

⁵⁰Jesus replied, "You believe because I told you that I saw you under the fig tree. You will see greater things than that." ⁵¹Jesus said to Nathanael, "I can guarantee this truth: You will see the sky open and God's angels going up and coming down to the Son of Man."

Jesus Changes Water into Wine

2 ¹Three days later a wedding took place in the city of Cana in Galilee. Jesus' mother was there. ²Jesus and his disciples had been invited too.

³When the wine was gone, Jesus' mother said to him, "They're out of wine."

⁴Jesus said to her, "Why did you come to me? My time has not yet come."

⁵His mother told the servers, "Do whatever he tells you."

⁶Six stone water jars were there. They were used for Jewish purification rituals. Each jar held 18 to 27 gallons.

⁷Jesus told the servers, "Fill the jars with water." The servers filled the jars to the brim. ⁸Jesus said to them, "Pour some, and take it to the person in charge." The servers did as they were told.

⁹The person in charge tasted the water that had become wine. He didn't know where it had come from, although the servers who had poured the water knew. The person in charge called the groom ¹⁰and said to him, "Everyone serves the best wine first. When people are drunk, the host serves cheap wine. But you have saved the best wine for now."

¹¹Cana in Galilee was the place where Jesus began to perform miracles. He made his glory public there, and his disciples believed in him.

¹²After this, Jesus, his mother, brothers, and disciples went to the city of Capernaum and stayed there for a few days.

Jesus Throws Merchants and Moneychangers out of the Temple Courtyard

¹³The Jewish Passover was near, so Jesus went to Jerusalem. ¹⁴He found those who were selling cattle, sheep, and pigeons in the temple courtyard. He also found moneychangers sitting there. ¹⁵He made a whip from small ropes and threw

everyone with their sheep and cattle out of the temple courtyard. He dumped the moneychangers' coins and knocked over their tables.

[16]He told those who sold pigeons, "Pick up this stuff, and get it out of here! Stop making my Father's house a marketplace!"

[17]His disciples remembered that Scripture said, "Devotion for your house will consume me."

[18]The Jews reacted by asking Jesus, "What miracle can you show us to justify what you're doing?"

[19]Jesus replied, "Tear down this temple, and I'll rebuild it in three days."

[20]The Jews said, "It took forty-six years to build this temple. Do you really think you're going to rebuild it in three days?"

[21]But the temple Jesus spoke about was his own body. [22]After he came back to life, his disciples remembered that he had said this. So they believed the Scripture and this statement that Jesus had made.

[23]While Jesus was in Jerusalem at the Passover festival, many people believed in him because they saw the miracles that he performed. [24]Jesus, however, was wary of these believers. He understood people [25]and didn't need anyone to tell him about human nature. He knew what people were really like.

A Conversation with Nicodemus

3[1]Nicodemus was a Pharisee and a member of the Jewish council. [2]He came to Jesus one night and said to him, "Rabbi, we know that God has sent you as a teacher. No one can perform the miracles you perform unless God is with him."

³Jesus replied to Nicodemus, "I can guarantee this truth: No one can see the kingdom of God without being born from above."

⁴Nicodemus asked him, "How can anyone be born when he's an old man? He can't go back inside his mother a second time to be born, can he?"

⁵Jesus answered Nicodemus, "I can guarantee this truth: No one can enter the kingdom of God without being born of water and the Spirit. ⁶Flesh and blood give birth to flesh and blood, but the Spirit gives birth to things that are spiritual. ⁷Don't be surprised when I tell you that all of you must be born from above. ⁸The wind blows wherever it pleases. You hear its sound, but you don't know where the wind comes from or where it's going. That's the way it is with everyone born of the Spirit."

Conversion—A Spiritual Rebirth

The Bible reveals that conversion is not simply changing habits, but completely changing the condition of our hearts. This spiritual rebirth is brought about by the Holy Spirit working through God's word. It takes place through a person's acceptance of Jesus as his or her real and only Savior (see also Jeremiah 31:18; Ezekiel 11:19; Joel 2:13; Romans 10:17; 1 Peter 1:23; 1 John 5:1).

---

⁹Nicodemus replied, "How can that be?"

¹⁰Jesus told Nicodemus, "You're a well-known teacher of Israel. Can't you understand this? ¹¹I can guarantee this truth: We know what we're

talking about, and we confirm what we've seen. Yet, you don't accept our message. ¹²If you don't believe me when I tell you about things on earth, how will you believe me when I tell you about things in heaven? ¹³No one has gone to heaven except the Son of Man, who came from heaven.

¹⁴"As Moses lifted up the snake on a pole in the desert, so the Son of Man must be lifted up. ¹⁵Then everyone who believes in him will have eternal life."

¹⁶God loved the world this way: He gave his only Son so that everyone who believes in him will not die but will have eternal life. ¹⁷God sent his Son into the world, not to condemn the world, but to save the world. ¹⁸Those who believe in him won't be condemned. But those who don't believe are already condemned because they don't believe in God's only Son.

Eternal Life

Some people say there are many ways to get into heaven. Who will be given eternal life in heaven? Does everyone automatically get to go to heaven? These verses reveal that only those who believe that Jesus is God and trust him as their real and only Savior will have eternal life in heaven.

The Good News

The Bible reveals that the Good News is the special revelation of what a loving and merciful God has done through Jesus—and still does for the salvation of humans today. This Good News freely offers sinful people the righteousness that only Jesus possesses. It saves everyone who trusts its promises (see also Ezekiel 33:11; Luke 4:18–19; Romans 1:16; 3:21–24; 1 Timothy 2:4).

¹⁹This is why people are condemned: The light came into the world. Yet, people loved the dark rather than the light because their actions were

evil. [20]People who do what is wrong hate the light and don't come to the light. They don't want their actions to be exposed. [21]But people who do what is true come to the light so that the things they do for God may be clearly seen.

John the Baptizer Talks about Christ

[22]Later, Jesus and his disciples went to the Judean countryside, where he spent some time with them and baptized people. [23]John was baptizing in Aenon, near Salim. Water was plentiful there. (People came to John to be baptized, [24]since John had not yet been put in prison.)

[25]Some of John's disciples had an argument with a Jew about purification ceremonies. [26]So they went to John and asked him, "Rabbi, do you remember the man you spoke so favorably about when he was with you on the other side of the Jordan River? Well, he's baptizing, and everyone is going to him!"

[27]John answered, "People can't receive anything unless it has been given to them from heaven. [28]You are witnesses that I said, 'I'm not the Messiah, but I've been sent ahead of him.'

[29]"The groom is the person to whom the bride belongs. The best man, who stands and listens to him, is overjoyed when the groom speaks. This is the joy that I feel. [30]He must increase in importance, while I must decrease in importance.

[31]"The person who comes from above is superior to everyone. I, a person from the earth, know nothing but what is on earth, and that's

all I can talk about. The person who comes from heaven is superior to everyone ³²and tells what he has seen and heard. Yet, no one accepts what he says. ³³I have accepted what that person said, and I have affirmed that God is truthful. ³⁴The man whom God has sent speaks God's message. After all, God gives him the Spirit without limit. ³⁵The Father loves his Son and has put everything in his power. ³⁶Whoever believes in the Son has eternal life, but whoever rejects the Son will not see life. Instead, he will see God's constant anger."

Faith
The Bible says that faith is a sinful person's acceptance of Jesus as his or her real and only Savior. Such acceptance includes complete reliance on Jesus' perfect life and sacrificial death for the forgiveness of sins and salvation. The Bible also reveals that this faith is not the result of anything a person does, but a work of the Holy Spirit. The person who endures in this faith to the end will have eternal life. Tragically, without such faith no salvation is possible (see also Matthew 24:13; John 1:12, 16; Acts 10:43; 16:31; 1 Corinthians 12:3; Galatians 2:16; 1 Peter 1:5).

A Samaritan Woman Meets Jesus at a Well

4 ¹Jesus knew that the Pharisees had heard that he was making and baptizing more disciples than John. ²(Actually, Jesus was not baptizing people. His disciples were.) ³So he left the Judean countryside and went back to Galilee.

⁴Jesus had to go through Samaria. ⁵He arrived at a city in Samaria called Sychar. Sychar was near the piece of land that Jacob had given to his son Joseph. ⁶Jacob's Well was there. Jesus sat down by

the well because he was tired from traveling. The time was about six o'clock in the evening.

⁷A Samaritan woman went to get some water. Jesus said to her, "Give me a drink of water." ⁸(His disciples had gone into the city to buy some food.)

⁹The Samaritan woman asked him, "How can a Jewish man like you ask a Samaritan woman like me for a drink of water?" (Jews, of course, don't associate with Samaritans.)

¹⁰Jesus replied to her, "If you only knew what God's gift is and who is asking you for a drink, you would have asked him for a drink. He would have given you living water."

¹¹The woman said to him, "Sir, you don't have anything to use to get water, and the well is deep. So where are you going to get this living water? ¹²You're not more important than our ancestor Jacob, are you? He gave us this well. He and his sons and his animals drank water from it."

¹³Jesus answered her, "Everyone who drinks this water will become thirsty again. ¹⁴But those who drink the water that I will give them will never become thirsty again. In fact, the water I will give them will become in them a spring that gushes up to eternal life."

¹⁵The woman told Jesus, "Sir, give me this water! Then I won't get thirsty or have to come here to get water."

¹⁶Jesus told her, "Go to your husband, and bring him here."

¹⁷The woman replied, "I don't have a husband."

Jesus told her, "You're right when you say that you don't have a husband. ¹⁸You've had five husbands, and the man you have now isn't your husband. You've told the truth."

¹⁹The woman said to Jesus, "I see that you're a prophet! ²⁰Our ancestors worshiped on this mountain. But you Jews say that people must worship in Jerusalem."

²¹Jesus told her, "Believe me. A time is coming when you Samaritans won't be worshiping the Father on this mountain or in Jerusalem. ²²You don't know what you're worshiping. We Jews know what we're worshiping, because salvation comes from the Jews. ²³Indeed, the time is coming, and it is now here, when the true worshipers will worship the Father in spirit and truth. The Father is looking for people like that to worship him. ²⁴God is a spirit. Those who worship him must worship in spirit and truth."

What Really Matters

Jesus was confronted by a woman at a well, and their conversation quickly turned to spiritual matters. While the woman wanted to debate where to worship God, Jesus settled the matter by telling her what really mattered: the condition of her heart. God is more interested in the condition of our hearts than he is in the size or location of our church building.

²⁵The woman said to him, "I know that the Messiah is coming. When he comes, he will tell us everything." (*Messiah* is the one called *Christ*.)

²⁶Jesus told her, "I am he, and I am speaking to you now."

²⁷At that time his disciples returned. They were surprised that he was talking to a woman. But

none of them asked him, "What do you want from her?" or "Why are you talking to her?"

²⁸Then the woman left her water jar and went back into the city. She told the people, ²⁹"Come with me, and meet a man who told me everything I've ever done. Could he be the Messiah?" ³⁰The people left the city and went to meet Jesus.

³¹Meanwhile, the disciples were urging him, "Rabbi, have something to eat."

³²Jesus told them, "I have food to eat that you don't know about."

³³The disciples asked each other, "Did someone bring him something to eat?"

³⁴Jesus told them, "My food is to do what the one who sent me wants me to do and to finish the work he has given me.

³⁵"Don't you say, 'In four more months the harvest will be here'? I'm telling you to look and see that the fields are ready to be harvested. ³⁶The person who harvests the crop is already getting paid. He is gathering grain for eternal life. So the person who plants the grain and the person who harvests it are happy together. ³⁷In this respect the saying is true: 'One person plants, and another person harvests.' ³⁸I have sent you to harvest a crop you have not worked for. Other people have done the hard work, and you have followed them in their work."

³⁹Many Samaritans in that city believed in Jesus because of the woman who said, "He told me everything I've ever done." ⁴⁰So when the Samaritans went to Jesus, they asked him to stay with them. He stayed in Samaria for two days. ⁴¹Many more Samaritans believed because of

what Jesus said. ⁴²They told the woman, "Our faith is no longer based on what you've said. We have heard him ourselves, and we know that he really is the savior of the world."

The Importance of Telling People about Jesus
Jesus used an example from agriculture to motivate us to tell people about him. People all around us are ready to respond to the Good News about him. Don't put off telling a close friend about Jesus because it never seems to be "the right time." Jesus said that now is the right time to tell others about him.

A Believing Official

(Matthew 8:5–13; Luke 7:1–10)

⁴³After spending two days in Samaria, Jesus left for Galilee. ⁴⁴Jesus had said that a prophet is not honored in his own country. ⁴⁵But when Jesus arrived in Galilee, the people of Galilee welcomed him. They had seen everything he had done at the festival in Jerusalem, since they, too, had attended the festival.

⁴⁶Jesus returned to the city of Cana in Galilee, where he had changed water into wine. A government official was in Cana. His son was sick in Capernaum. ⁴⁷The official heard that Jesus had returned from Judea to Galilee. So he went to Jesus and asked him to go to Capernaum with him to heal his son who was about to die.

⁴⁸Jesus told the official, "If people don't see miracles and amazing things, they won't believe."

⁴⁹The official said to him, "Sir, come with me before my little boy dies."

⁵⁰Jesus told him, "Go home. Your son will live." The man believed what Jesus told him and left.

⁵¹While the official was on his way to Capernaum, his servants met him and told him that his boy was alive. ⁵²The official asked them at what time his son got better. His servants told him, "The fever left him yesterday evening at seven o'clock." ⁵³Then the boy's father realized that it was the same time that Jesus had told him, "Your son will live." So the official and his entire family became believers.

⁵⁴This was the second miracle that Jesus performed after he had come back from Judea to Galilee.

Jesus Cures a Man at the Bethesda Pool

5¹Later, Jesus went to Jerusalem for a Jewish festival. ²Near Sheep Gate in Jerusalem was a pool called *Bethesda* in Hebrew. It had five porches. ³Under these porches a large number of sick people—people who were blind, lame, or paralyzed—used to lie. ⁵One man, who had been sick for 38 years, was lying there. ⁶Jesus saw the man lying there and knew that he had been sick for a long time. So Jesus asked the man, "Would you like to get well?"

⁷The sick man answered Jesus, "Sir, I don't have anyone to put me into the pool when the water is stirred. While I'm trying to get there, someone else steps into the pool ahead of me."

⁸Jesus told the man, "Get up, pick up your cot, and walk." ⁹The man immediately became well, picked up his cot, and walked.

That happened on a day of worship. ¹⁰So the Jews told the man who had been healed, "This is a day of worship. You're not allowed to carry your cot today."

¹¹The man replied, "The man who made me well told me to pick up my cot and walk."

¹²The Jews asked him, "Who is the man who told you to pick it up and walk?" ¹³But the man who had been healed didn't know who Jesus was. (Jesus had withdrawn from the crowd.)

¹⁴Later, Jesus met the man in the temple courtyard and told him, "You're well now. Stop sinning so that something worse doesn't happen to you."

¹⁵The man went back to the Jews and told them that Jesus was the man who had made him well.

The Son Is Equal to the Father

¹⁶The Jews began to persecute Jesus because he kept healing people on the day of worship. ¹⁷Jesus replied to them, "My Father is working right now, and so am I."

¹⁸His reply made the Jews more intent on killing him. Not only did he break the laws about the day of worship, but also he made himself equal to God when he said repeatedly that God was his Father.

¹⁹Jesus said to the Jews, "I can guarantee this truth: The Son cannot do anything on his own. He can do only what he sees the Father doing. Indeed, the Son does exactly what the Father does. ²⁰The

Father loves the Son and shows him everything he is doing. The Father will show him even greater things to do than these things so that you will be amazed. ²¹In the same way that the Father brings back the dead and gives them life, the Son gives life to anyone he chooses.

²²"The Father doesn't judge anyone. He has entrusted judgment entirely to the Son ²³so that everyone will honor the Son as they honor the Father. Whoever doesn't honor the Son doesn't honor the Father who sent him. ²⁴I can guarantee this truth: Those who listen to what I say and believe in the one who sent me will have eternal life. They won't be judged because they have already passed from death to life."

The Savior

The Bible says that Jesus is the Son of God and equal to the Father in every respect. He's also the son of the virgin Mary. He became human in order to save us. He satisfied the demands of the law in Moses' teachings for everyone by keeping God's commandments for us, and took the punishment we deserved for our sins by suffering and dying in our place on the cross. He came back to life from the dead and lives today. He will return visibly at the world's end to judge everyone (see also Matthew 1:18–25; 10:30; 14:9; Acts 1:11; 10:42; Romans 4:25; Galatians 3:13; 4:4, 5; 1 Peter 2:22, 24; 1 John 2:1–2).

The Triune God

The Bible reveals that the one true God is triune—one God in three persons: Father, Son, and Holy Spirit. These three persons are equal in all things. To ignore and deny one is to disavow all. God is the one who creates, the one who saves, and the one who makes people holy (see also Genesis 1:1; Deuteronomy 6:4; Matthew 28:19; Romans 15:13; 1 John 2:1–2, 23).

---

²⁵"I can guarantee this truth: A time is coming (and is now here) when the dead will hear the

voice of the Son of God and those who respond to it will live. ²⁶The Father is the source of life, and he has enabled the Son to be the source of life too.

²⁷"He has also given the Son authority to pass judgment because he is the Son of Man. ²⁸Don't be surprised at what I've just said. A time is coming when all the dead will hear his voice, ²⁹and they will come out of their tombs. Those who have done good will come back to life and live. But those who have done evil will come back to life and will be judged. ³⁰I can't do anything on my own. As I listen to the Father, I make my judgments. My judgments are right because I don't try to do what I want but what the one who sent me wants."

Life after Death

The Bible teaches that the body, which at the time of death is separated from the believer's soul, will be brought back to life on the Last Day and reunited with the soul. All who believe that Jesus is God and trusts him as their only and real Savior will be given eternal life in heaven, while all unbelievers will be judged and sent into eternal condemnation (see also Matthew 25:31–46).

³¹"If I testify on my own behalf, what I say isn't true. ³²Someone else testifies on my behalf, and I know that what he says about me is true. ³³You sent people to John the Baptizer, and he testified to the truth. ³⁴But I don't depend on human testimony. I'm telling you this to save you. ³⁵John was a lamp that gave off brilliant light. For a time you enjoyed the pleasure of his light. ³⁶But I have something that testifies more favorably on my behalf than John's testimony. The tasks that the

Father gave me to carry out, these tasks which I perform, testify on my behalf. They prove that the Father has sent me. ³⁷The Father who sent me testifies on my behalf. You have never heard his voice, and you have never seen his form. ³⁸So you don't have the Father's message within you, because you don't believe in the person he has sent. ³⁹You study the Scriptures in detail because you think you have the source of eternal life in them. These Scriptures testify on my behalf. ⁴⁰Yet, you don't want to come to me to get eternal life.

The Bible

The Bible in all its words is God's revelation to humans. As a result, all the facts revealed in it are absolutely true and without error. The Bible interprets itself. It's the only divine truth known on earth and should be diligently heard and studied. Most importantly, it will save everyone who trusts its message of salvation (see also Luke 11:28; 1 Corinthians 2:13; 2 Peter 1:21).

Many people still ask, "But isn't the Bible filled with myths and contradictions?" This question is often asked by people who have never really read the Bible! In fact, just the opposite is true. The Bible is the most studied and documented book in history. God's revelation has been scrutinized for centuries. At the beginning of the twentieth century, many skeptics and liberal theologians pronounced that God's word was neither historical nor factual, but rather allegory, myth, and fable. With the advent of modern archaeology, many people expected that the Bible would prove to be a mere human document filled with errors. However, over the past hundred years, archaeology has proven just the opposite and has validated the truthfulness of the Bible down to some of the smallest details.

If the Bible is to be considered God's revelation to humans—a word that is reliable, true, accurate, and life-changing—then it must meet certain requirements. First, it must be transmitted accurately from the time it was originally written to the present, so that we have an accurate representation of what God has said and done. Second, it must be correct when it deals with historical persons and events. Third, any revelation from God should be without any scientific problems that would indicate that it was authored by humans.

The Bible meets all these criteria and more! The text of the Bible has been transmitted accurately for nearly three thousand years. There is more evidence for the accuracy of the New Testament than all other historical writings. The New Testament alone has more that 25,000 handwritten copies that are 99 percent in agreement with one another. Remarkable!

⁴¹"I don't accept praise from humans. ⁴²But I know what kind of people you are. You don't have any love for God. ⁴³I have come with the authority my Father has given me, but you don't accept me. If someone else comes with his own authority, you will accept him. ⁴⁴How can you believe when you accept each other's praise and don't look for the praise that comes from the only God?

⁴⁵"Don't think that I will accuse you in the presence of the Father. Moses, the one you trust, is already accusing you. ⁴⁶If you really believed Moses, you would believe me. Moses wrote about me. ⁴⁷If you don't believe what Moses wrote, how will you ever believe what I say?"

Jesus Feeds More Than Five Thousand
(Matthew 14:13–21; Mark 6:30–44; Luke 9:10–17)

6 ¹Jesus later crossed to the other side of the Sea of Galilee (or the Sea of Tiberias). ²A large crowd followed him because they saw the miracles that he performed for the sick. ³Jesus went up a mountain and sat with his disciples. ⁴The time for the Jewish Passover festival was near.

⁵As Jesus saw a large crowd coming to him, he said to Philip, "Where can we buy bread for these people to eat?" ⁶Jesus asked this question to test him. He already knew what he was going to do.

⁷Philip answered, "We would need about a year's wages to buy enough bread for each of them to have a piece."

⁸One of Jesus' disciples, Andrew, who was Simon Peter's brother, told him, ⁹"A boy who has five loaves of barley bread and two small fish is here. But they won't go very far for so many people."

¹⁰Jesus said, "Have the people sit down."

The people had plenty of grass to sit on. (There were about 5,000 men in the crowd.)

¹¹Jesus took the loaves, gave thanks, and distributed them to the people who were sitting there. He did the same thing with the fish. All the people ate as much as they wanted.

¹²When the people were full, Jesus told his disciples, "Gather the leftover pieces so that nothing will be wasted." ¹³The disciples gathered the leftover pieces of bread and filled twelve baskets.

¹⁴When the people saw the miracle Jesus performed, they said, "This man is certainly the prophet who is to come into the world." ¹⁵Jesus realized that the people intended to take him by force and make him king. So he returned to the mountain by himself.

Jesus Walks on the Sea
(Matthew 14:22–33; Mark 6:45–52)

¹⁶When evening came, his disciples went to the sea. ¹⁷They got into a boat and started to cross the sea to the city of Capernaum. By this time it was dark, and Jesus had not yet come to them.

¹⁸A strong wind started to blow and stir up the sea.

¹⁹After they had rowed three or four miles, they saw Jesus walking on the sea. He was coming near the boat, and they became terrified.

²⁰Jesus told them, "It's me. Don't be afraid!"

²¹So they were willing to help Jesus into the boat. Immediately, the boat reached the shore where they were going.

Jesus Is the Bread of Life

²²On the next day the people were still on the other side of the sea. They noticed that only one boat was there and that Jesus had not stepped into that boat with his disciples. The disciples had gone away without him. ²³Other boats from Tiberias arrived near the place where they had eaten the bread after the Lord gave thanks. ²⁴When the people saw that neither Jesus nor his disciples were there, they got into these boats and went to the city of Capernaum to look for Jesus. ²⁵When they found him on the other side of the sea, they asked him, "Rabbi, when did you get here?"

²⁶Jesus replied to them, "I can guarantee this truth: You're not looking for me because you saw miracles. You are looking for me because you ate as much of those loaves as you wanted. ²⁷Don't work for food that spoils. Instead, work for the food that lasts into eternal life. This is the food the Son of Man will give you. After all, the Father has placed his seal of approval on him."

²⁸The people asked Jesus, "What does God want us to do?"

²⁹Jesus replied to them, "God wants to do something for you so that you believe in the one whom he has sent."

³⁰The people asked him, "What miracle are you going to perform so that we can see it and believe in you? What are you going to do? ³¹Our ancestors ate the manna in the desert. Scripture says, 'He gave them bread from heaven to eat.'"

³²Jesus said to them, "I can guarantee this truth: Moses didn't give you bread from heaven, but my Father gives you the true bread from heaven. ³³God's bread is the man who comes from heaven and gives life to the world."

³⁴They said to him, "Sir, give us this bread all the time."

³⁵Jesus told them, "I am the bread of life. Whoever comes to me will never become hungry, and whoever believes in me will never become thirsty. ³⁶I've told you that you have seen me. However, you don't believe in me. ³⁷Everyone whom the Father gives me will come to me. I will never turn away anyone who comes to me. ³⁸I haven't come from heaven to do what I want to do. I've come to do what the one who sent me wants me to do. ³⁹The one who sent me doesn't want me to lose any of those he gave me. He wants me to bring them back to life on the last day. ⁴⁰My Father wants all those who see the Son and believe in him to have eternal life. He wants me to bring them back to life on the last day."

Selfishness

Following our own way can lead us down the wrong road. With all of heaven and earth at his command, Jesus did not demand his own way. Instead, he lived according to God's plan for his life. We must choose God's way over our own desires. Then we can get ready to experience his blessings in every area of our lives.

What Can Following Jesus Do for My Daily Life?

Built into each person is the need to do something that really makes a difference. Life without purpose is not truly living. Jesus offers real purpose for daily living. His purposes are both temporal (for this period of time) and eternal. It's exciting to realize that we can have a purpose for living that transcends a paycheck or a product.

Following Jesus can also fill a person's life with real joy—internal peace and confidence that are unaffected by external problems. Joy is the by-product of a living relationship with Jesus.

Following Jesus can also benefit one's daily life in terms of healthy relationships. When a person is secure because of his or her faith in Jesus, the need to control or manipulate other people comes to an end. There's real joy and satisfaction in caring for another person, not because of what that person can give or do for you, but because of the love that Jesus has shown you. Through Jesus we can have significant, meaningful relationships with God and others.

---

⁴¹The Jews began to criticize Jesus for saying, "I am the bread that came from heaven." ⁴²They asked, "Isn't this man Jesus, Joseph's son? Don't we know his father and mother? How can he say now, 'I came from heaven'?"

⁴³Jesus responded, "Stop criticizing me! ⁴⁴People cannot come to me unless the Father who sent me brings them to me. I will bring these people back to life on the last day. ⁴⁵The prophets wrote, 'God will teach everyone.' Those who do what they have learned from the Father come to me. ⁴⁶I'm saying that no one has seen the Father. Only the one who is from God has seen the Father.

⁴⁷I can guarantee this truth: Every believer has eternal life.

⁴⁸"I am the bread of life. ⁴⁹Your ancestors ate the manna in the desert and died. ⁵⁰This is the bread that comes from heaven so that whoever eats it won't die. ⁵¹I am the living bread that came from heaven. Whoever eats this bread will live forever. The bread I will give to bring life to the world is my flesh."

⁵²The Jews began to quarrel with each other. They said, "How can this man give us his flesh to eat?"

⁵³Jesus told them, "I can guarantee this truth: If you don't eat the flesh of the Son of Man and drink his blood, you don't have the source of life in you. ⁵⁴Those who eat my flesh and drink my blood have eternal life, and I will bring them back to life on the last day. ⁵⁵My flesh is true food, and my blood is true drink. ⁵⁶Those who eat my flesh and drink my blood live in me, and I live in them. ⁵⁷The Father who has life sent me, and I live because of the Father. So those who feed on me will live because of me. ⁵⁸This is the bread that came from heaven. It is not like the bread your ancestors ate. They eventually died. Those who eat this bread will live forever."

⁵⁹Jesus said this while he was teaching in a synagogue in Capernaum. ⁶⁰When many of Jesus' disciples heard him, they said, "What he says is hard to accept. Who wants to listen to him anymore?"

⁶¹Jesus was aware that his disciples were criticizing his message. So Jesus asked them, "Did what I say make you lose faith? ⁶²What if you see the Son of Man go where he was before? ⁶³Life is spiritual. Your physical existence doesn't con-

tribute to that life. The words that I have spoken to you are spiritual. They are life. [64]But some of you don't believe." Jesus knew from the beginning those who wouldn't believe and the one who would betray him. [65]So he added, "That is why I told you that people cannot come to me unless the Father provides the way."

[66]Jesus' speech made many of his disciples go back to the lives they had led before they followed Jesus. [67]So Jesus asked the twelve apostles, "Do you want to leave me too?"

[68]Simon Peter answered Jesus, "Lord, to what person could we go? Your words give eternal life. [69]Besides, we believe and know that you are the Holy One of God."

[70]Jesus replied, "I chose all twelve of you. Yet, one of you is a devil." [71]Jesus meant Judas, son of Simon Iscariot. Judas, who was one of the twelve apostles, would later betray Jesus.

Eternal Life

Some people say there are many ways to get into heaven. But in this verse, Peter states the fact that no one but Jesus offers any real hope for eternal life. Several of Jesus' followers had decided his teachings were too hard, and they chose not to follow him any longer. But when Jesus asked the rest of his followers if they wanted to leave him, too, Peter said there was nowhere else to go: only Jesus' words give eternal life. Nothing has changed since then; there is still no other way to have peace with God and enjoy life after death. Following Jesus may be difficult at times, but it's the only option.

Jesus Goes to the Festival of Booths

7 [1]Jesus later traveled throughout Galilee. He didn't want to travel in Judea because Jews there wanted to kill him. ²The time for the Jewish Festival of Booths was near. ³So Jesus' brothers told him, "Leave this place, and go to Judea so that your disciples can see the things that you're doing. ⁴No one does things secretly when he wants to be known publicly. If you do these things, you should let the world see you." ⁵Even his brothers didn't believe in him.

⁶Jesus told them, "Now is not the right time for me to go. Any time is right for you. ⁷The world cannot hate you, but it hates me because I say that what everyone does is evil. ⁸Go to the festival. I'm not going to this festival right now. Now is not the right time for me to go."

⁹After saying this, Jesus stayed in Galilee. ¹⁰But after his brothers had gone to the festival, Jesus went. He didn't go publicly but secretly.

¹¹The Jews were looking for Jesus in the crowd at the festival. They kept asking, "Where is that man?" ¹²The crowds argued about Jesus. Some people said, "He's a good man," while others said, "No he isn't. He deceives the people." ¹³Yet, no one would talk openly about him because they were afraid of the Jews.

¹⁴When the festival was half over, Jesus went to the temple courtyard and began to teach. ¹⁵The Jews were surprised and asked, "How can this man be so educated when he hasn't gone to school?"

¹⁶Jesus responded to them, "What I teach doesn't come from me but from the one who sent me. ¹⁷Those who want to follow the will of God will know if what I teach is from God or if I teach my own thoughts. ¹⁸Those who speak their own

thoughts are looking for their own glory. But the man who wants to bring glory to the one who sent him is a true teacher and doesn't have dishonest motives. ¹⁹Didn't Moses give you his teachings? Yet, none of you does what Moses taught you. So why do you want to kill me?"

²⁰The crowd answered, "You're possessed by a demon! Who wants to kill you?"

²¹Jesus answered them, "I performed one miracle, and all of you are surprised by it. ²²Moses gave you the teaching about circumcision (although it didn't come from Moses but from our ancestors). So you circumcise a male on a day of worship. ²³If you circumcise a male on the day of worship to follow Moses' Teachings, why are you angry with me because I made a man entirely well on the day of worship? ²⁴Stop judging by outward appearance! Instead, judge correctly."

²⁵Some of the people who lived in Jerusalem said, "Isn't this the man they want to kill? ²⁶But look at this! He's speaking in public, and no one is saying anything to him! Can it be that the rulers really know that this man is the Messiah? ²⁷However, we know where this man comes from. When the Christ comes, no one will know where he is from."

²⁸Then, while Jesus was teaching in the temple courtyard, he said loudly, "You know me, and you know where I come from. I didn't decide to come on my own. The one who sent me is true. He's the one you don't know. ²⁹I know him because I am from him and he sent me."

³⁰The Jews tried to arrest him but couldn't because his time had not yet come.

³¹However, many people in the crowd believed in him. They asked, "When the Messiah comes, will he perform more miracles than this man has?"

³²The Pharisees heard the crowd saying things like this about him. So the chief priests and the Pharisees sent temple guards to arrest Jesus.

³³Jesus said, "I will still be with you for a little while. Then I'll go to the one who sent me. ³⁴You will look for me, but you won't find me. You can't go where I'm going."

³⁵The Jews said among themselves, "Where does this man intend to go so that we won't find him? Does he mean that he'll live with the Jews who are scattered among the Greeks and that he'll teach the Greeks? ³⁶What does he mean when he says, 'You will look for me, but you won't find me,' and 'You can't go where I'm going'?"

³⁷On the last and most important day of the festival, Jesus was standing in the temple courtyard. He said loudly, "Whoever is thirsty must come to me to drink. ³⁸As Scripture says, 'Streams of living water will flow from deep within the person who believes in me.'" ³⁹Jesus said this about the Spirit, whom his believers would receive. The Spirit was not yet evident, as it would be after Jesus had been glorified.

⁴⁰After some of the crowd heard Jesus say these words, they said, "This man is certainly the prophet." ⁴¹Other people said, "This man is the Messiah." Still other people asked, "How can the Messiah come from Galilee? ⁴²Doesn't Scripture say that the Messiah will come from the descendants of David and from the village of Bethlehem,

where David lived?" ⁴³So the people were divided because of Jesus. ⁴⁴Some of them wanted to arrest him, but they couldn't.

⁴⁵When the temple guards returned, the chief priests and Pharisees asked them, "Why didn't you bring Jesus?"

⁴⁶The temple guards answered, "No human has ever spoken like this man."

⁴⁷The Pharisees asked the temple guards, "Have you been deceived too? ⁴⁸Has any ruler or any Pharisee believed in him? ⁴⁹This crowd is cursed because it doesn't know Moses' Teachings."

⁵⁰One of those Pharisees was Nicodemus, who had previously visited Jesus. Nicodemus asked them, ⁵¹"Do Moses' Teachings enable us to judge a person without first hearing that person's side of the story? We can't judge a person without finding out what that person has done."

⁵²They asked Nicodemus, "Are you saying this because you're from Galilee? Study the Scriptures, and you'll see that no prophet comes from Galilee."

⁵³Then each of them went home.

A Woman Caught in Adultery

8 ¹Jesus went to the Mount of Olives. ²Early the next morning he returned to the temple courtyard. All the people went to him, so he sat down and began to teach them.

³The scribes and the Pharisees brought a woman who had been caught committing adultery. They made her stand in front of everyone

[4]and asked Jesus, "Teacher, we caught this woman in the act of adultery. [5]In his teachings, Moses ordered us to stone women like this to death. What do you say?" [6]They asked this to test him. They wanted to find a reason to bring charges against him.

Jesus bent down and used his finger to write on the ground. [7]When they persisted in asking him questions, he straightened up and said, "The person who is sinless should be the first to throw a stone at her." [8]Then he bent down again and continued writing on the ground.

[9]One by one, beginning with the older men, the scribes and Pharisees left. Jesus was left alone with the woman. [10]Then Jesus straightened up and asked her, "Where did they go? Has anyone condemned you?"

[11]The woman answered, "No one, sir."

Jesus said, "I don't condemn you either. Go! From now on don't sin."

Jesus Speaks with the Pharisees about His Father

[12]Jesus spoke to the Pharisees again. He said, "I am the light of the world. Whoever follows me will have a life filled with light and will never live in the dark."

Darkness and Light

Darkness makes it difficult to see where we're going. Spiritual darkness makes it impossible to know how to get to God. Through Jesus we have a solution to the problem of spiritual darkness. Because of him, we have "a

Hope for Today

life filled with light." Through Jesus we can have a significant, meaningful, and eternal relationship with God.

---

¹³The Pharisees said to him, "You testify on your own behalf, so your testimony isn't true."

¹⁴Jesus replied to them, "Even if I testify on my own behalf, my testimony is true because I know where I came from and where I'm going. However, you don't know where I came from or where I'm going. ¹⁵You judge the way humans do. I don't judge anyone. ¹⁶Even if I do judge, my judgment is valid because I don't make it on my own. I make my judgment with the Father who sent me. ¹⁷Your own teachings say that the testimony of two people is true. ¹⁸I testify on my own behalf, and so does the Father who sent me."

¹⁹The Pharisees asked him, "Where is your father?"

Jesus replied, "You don't know me or my Father. If you knew me, you would also know my Father."

²⁰Jesus spoke these words while he was teaching in the treasury area of the temple courtyard. No one arrested him, because his time had not yet come.

²¹Jesus spoke to the Pharisees again. He said, "I'm going away, and you'll look for me. But you will die because of your sin. You can't go where I'm going."

²²Then the Jews asked, "Is he going to kill himself? Is that what he means when he says, 'You can't go where I'm going'?"

²³Jesus said to them, "You're from below. I'm from above. You're from this world. I'm not from

this world. ²⁴For this reason I told you that you'll die because of your sins. If you don't believe that I am the one, you'll die because of your sins."

²⁵The Jews asked him, "Who did you say you are?"

Jesus told them, "I am who I said I was from the beginning. ²⁶I have a lot I could say about you and a lot I could condemn you for. But the one who sent me is true. So I tell the world exactly what he has told me." ²⁷(The Jews didn't know that he was talking to them about the Father.)

²⁸So Jesus told them, "When you have lifted up the Son of Man, then you'll know that I am the one and that I can't do anything on my own. Instead, I speak as the Father taught me. ²⁹Besides, the one who sent me is with me. He hasn't left me by myself. I always do what pleases him."

³⁰As Jesus was saying this, many people believed in him. ³¹So Jesus said to those Jews who believed in him, "If you live by what I say, you are truly my disciples. ³²You will know the truth, and the truth will set you free."

Sin

Whether you learned about slavery in history class or from your family's own history, you know that the master determined nearly every aspect of life for his or her slaves. Jesus told the Jews that people who sin are slaves to sin. His words are still true: Sin can ruin your life and make all your decisions for you—if you let it. Don't underestimate the power of sin!

The Church—The Community of Believers

The Bible reveals that there is an *invisible* church that consists of all who truly accept Jesus as their real and only Savior. This church is one, Jesus is its only Head and Lord, and all members thereof enjoy equal rights. This church may be found wherever the Good News of Jesus is known. This church will endure forever.

Hope for Today

The Bible also teaches that there is a *visible* church, consisting of everyone who professes the Christian faith and gathers about God's word. Sad to say, because of corrupt human nature, there will always be hypocrites and defenders of false teachings and unchristian practices in the church. Therefore, it's the duty of every sincere Christian to search for and unite with that part of the *visible* church that stands for the pure preaching and right practice of God's word (see also Isaiah 55:10–11; Matthew 13:47–48; 15:9; 16:18; 22:2–14; Luke 17:20–21; John 18:36; Romans 16:17; 1 Corinthians 11:18; 12:13; 2 Corinthians 6:14–18; Ephesians 1:22–23; 2:19–22; 2 Thessalonians 3:6, 14).

³³They replied to Jesus, "We are Abraham's descendants, and we've never been anyone's slaves. So how can you say that we will be set free?"

³⁴Jesus answered them, "I can guarantee this truth: Whoever lives a sinful life is a slave to sin. ³⁵A slave doesn't live in the home forever, but a son does. ³⁶So if the Son sets you free, you will be absolutely free.

³⁷I know that you're Abraham's descendants. However, you want to kill me because you don't like what I'm saying. ³⁸What I'm saying is what I have seen in my Father's presence. But you do what you've heard from your father."

³⁹The Jews replied to Jesus, "Abraham is our father."

Jesus told them, "If you were Abraham's children, you would do what Abraham did. ⁴⁰I am a man who has told you the truth that I heard from God. But now you want to kill me. Abraham wouldn't have done that. ⁴¹You're doing what your father does."

The Jews said to Jesus, "We're not illegitimate children. God is our only Father."

⁴²Jesus told them, "If God were your Father, you would love me. After all, I'm here, and I came from God. I didn't come on my own. Instead, God sent me. ⁴³Why don't you understand the language I use? Is it because you can't understand the words I use? ⁴⁴You come from your father, the devil, and you desire to do what your father wants you to do. The devil was a murderer from the beginning. He has never been truthful. He doesn't know what the truth is. Whenever he tells a lie, he's doing what comes naturally to him. He's a liar and the father of lies. ⁴⁵So you don't believe me because I tell the truth. ⁴⁶Can any of you convict me of committing a sin? If I'm telling the truth, why don't you believe me? ⁴⁷The person who belongs to God understands what God says. You don't understand because you don't belong to God."

⁴⁸The Jews replied to Jesus, "Aren't we right when we say that you're a Samaritan and that you're possessed by a demon?"

⁴⁹Jesus answered, "I'm not possessed. I honor my Father, but you dishonor me. ⁵⁰I don't want my own glory. But there is someone who wants it, and he is the judge. ⁵¹I can guarantee this truth: Whoever obeys what I say will never see death."

⁵²The Jews told Jesus, "Now we know that you're possessed by a demon. Abraham died, and so did the prophets, but you say, 'Whoever does what I say will never taste death.' ⁵³Are you greater than our father Abraham, who died? The prophets have also died. Who do you think you are?"

⁵⁴Jesus said, "If I bring glory to myself, my glory is nothing. My Father is the one who gives

me glory, and you say that he is your God. ⁵⁵Yet, you haven't known him. However, I know him. If I would say that I didn't know him, I would be a liar like all of you. But I do know him, and I do what he says. ⁵⁶Your father Abraham was pleased to see that my day was coming. He saw it and was happy."

⁵⁷The Jews said to Jesus, "You're not even fifty years old. How could you have seen Abraham?"

⁵⁸Jesus told them, "I can guarantee this truth: Before Abraham was ever born, I am."

⁵⁹Then some of the Jews picked up stones to throw at Jesus. However, Jesus was concealed, and he left the temple courtyard.

Jesus Gives Sight to a Blind Man

9 ¹As Jesus walked along, he saw a man who had been born blind. ²His disciples asked him, "Rabbi, why was this man born blind? Did he or his parents sin?"

³Jesus answered, "Neither this man nor his parents sinned. Instead, he was born blind so that God could show what he can do for him. ⁴We must do what the one who sent me wants us to do while it is day. The night when no one can do anything is coming. ⁵As long as I'm in the world, I'm light for the world."

⁶After Jesus said this, he spit on the ground and mixed the spit with dirt. Then he smeared it on the man's eyes ⁷and told him, "Wash it off in the pool of Siloam." (*Siloam* means "sent.") The

blind man washed it off and returned. He was able to see.

⁸His neighbors and those who had previously seen him begging asked, "Isn't this the man who used to sit and beg?"

⁹Some of them said, "He's the one." Others said, "No, he isn't, but he looks like him." But the man himself said, "I am the one."

¹⁰So they asked him, "How did you receive your sight?"

¹¹He replied, "The man people call Jesus mixed some spit with dirt, smeared it on my eyes, and told me, 'Go to Siloam, and wash it off.' So I went there, washed it off, and received my sight."

¹²They asked him, "Where is that man?"

The man answered, "I don't know."

¹³Some people brought the man who had been blind to the Pharisees. ¹⁴The day when Jesus mixed the spit and dirt and gave the man sight was a day of worship. ¹⁵So the Pharisees asked the man again how he received his sight.

The man told the Pharisees, "He put a mixture of spit and dirt on my eyes. I washed it off, and now I can see."

Guilt

Sin has an amazing way of blinding us to our guilt. The Pharisees were religious leaders who refused to see their own spiritual blindness. Their hypocrisy caused them to believe that they were good people when they were really quite sinful. Be careful that you don't overlook your sin and falsely believe that you are free from guilt.

---

¹⁶Some of the Pharisees said, "The man who did this is not from God because he doesn't follow the

traditions for the day of worship." Other Pharisees asked, "How can a man who is a sinner perform miracles like these?" So the Pharisees were divided in their opinions.

¹⁷They asked the man who had been born blind another question: "What do you say about the man who gave you sight?"

The man answered, "He's a prophet."

¹⁸Until they talked to the man's parents, the Jews didn't believe that the man had been blind and had been given sight. ¹⁹They asked his parents, "Is this your son, the one you say was born blind? Why can he see now?"

²⁰His parents replied, "We know that he's our son and that he was born blind. ²¹But we don't know how he got his sight or who gave it to him. You'll have to ask him. He's old enough to answer for himself." ²²(His parents said this because they were afraid of the Jews. The Jews had already agreed to put anyone who acknowledged that Jesus was the Christ out of the synagogue. ²³That's why his parents said, "You'll have to ask him. He's old enough.")

²⁴So once again the Jews called the man who had been blind. They told him, "Give glory to God. We know that this man who gave you sight is a sinner."

²⁵The man responded, "I don't know if he's a sinner or not. But I do know one thing. I used to be blind, but now I can see."

²⁶The Jews asked him, "What did he do to you? How did he give you sight?"

²⁷The man replied, "I've already told you, but you didn't listen. Why do you want to hear the

story again? Do you want to become his disciples too?"

²⁸The Jews yelled at him, "You're his disciple, but we're Moses' disciples. ²⁹We know that God spoke to Moses, but we don't know where this man came from."

³⁰The man replied to them, "That's amazing! You don't know where he's from. Yet, he gave me sight. ³¹We know that God doesn't listen to sinners. Instead, he listens to people who are devout and who do what he wants. ³²Since the beginning of time, no one has ever heard of anyone giving sight to a person born blind. ³³If this man were not from God, he couldn't do anything like that."

³⁴The Jews answered him, "You were born full of sin. Do you think you can teach us?" Then they threw him out of the synagogue.

³⁵Jesus heard that the Jews had thrown the man out of the synagogue. So when Jesus found the man, he asked him, "Do you believe in the Son of Man?"

³⁶The man replied, "Sir, tell me who he is so that I can believe in him."

³⁷Jesus told him, "You've seen him. He is the person who is now talking with you."

³⁸The man bowed in front of Jesus and said, "I believe, Lord."

³⁹Then Jesus said, "I have come into this world to judge: Blind people will be given sight, and those who can see will become blind."

⁴⁰Some Pharisees who were with Jesus heard this. So they asked him, "Do you think we're blind?"

⁴¹Jesus told them, "If you were blind, you wouldn't be sinners. But now you say, 'We see,' so you continue to be sinners."

Jesus, the Good Shepherd

10 ¹"I can guarantee this truth: The person who doesn't enter the sheep pen through the gate but climbs in somewhere else is a thief or a robber. ²But the one who enters through the gate is the shepherd. ³The gatekeeper opens the gate for him, and the sheep respond to his voice. He calls his sheep by name and leads them out of the pen. ⁴After he has brought out all his sheep, he walks ahead of them. The sheep follow him because they recognize his voice. ⁵They won't follow a stranger. Instead, they will run away from a stranger because they don't recognize his voice." ⁶Jesus used this illustration as he talked to the people, but they didn't understand what he meant.

⁷Jesus emphasized, "I can guarantee this truth: I am the gate for the sheep. ⁸All who came before I did were thieves or robbers. However, the sheep didn't respond to them. ⁹I am the gate. Those who enter the sheep pen through me will be saved. They will go in and out of the sheep pen and find food. ¹⁰A thief comes to steal, kill, and destroy. But I came so that my sheep will have life and so that they will have everything they need.

Jesus

Getting locked out of your house is frustrating. You have to wait for help in order to get inside. In John 10, Jesus provides help when we are "spiritually" locked out of God's presence. Jesus said that he is the gate and whoever enters into a relationship with the one true God through him will be saved. Jesus promised never to lock us out.

[11]"I am the good shepherd. The good shepherd gives his life for the sheep. [12]A hired hand isn't a shepherd and doesn't own the sheep. When he sees a wolf coming, he abandons the sheep and quickly runs away. So the wolf drags the sheep away and scatters the flock. [13]The hired hand is concerned about what he's going to get paid and not about the sheep.

[14]"I am the good shepherd. I know my sheep as the Father knows me. My sheep know me as I know the Father. [15]So I give my life for my sheep. [16]I also have other sheep that are not from this pen. I must lead them. They, too, will respond to my voice. So they will be one flock with one shepherd. [17]The Father loves me because I give my life in order to take it back again. [18]No one takes my life from me. I give my life of my own free will. I have the authority to give my life, and I have the authority to take my life back again. This is what my Father ordered me to do."

[19]The Jews were divided because of what Jesus said. [20]Many of them said, "He's possessed by a demon! He's crazy! Why do you listen to him?" [21]Others said, "No one talks like this if he's possessed by a demon. Can a demon give sight to the blind?"

The Jews Reject Jesus

²²The Festival of the Dedication of the Temple took place in Jerusalem during the winter. ²³Jesus was walking on Solomon's porch in the temple courtyard. ²⁴The Jews surrounded him. They asked him, "How long will you keep us in suspense? If you are the Messiah, tell us plainly."

²⁵Jesus answered them, "I've told you, but you don't believe me. The things that I do in my Father's name testify on my behalf. ²⁶However, you don't believe because you're not my sheep. ²⁷My sheep respond to my voice, and I know who they are. They follow me, ²⁸and I give them eternal life. They will never be lost, and no one will tear them away from me. ²⁹My Father, who gave them to me, is greater than everyone else, and no one can tear them away from my Father. ³⁰The Father and I are one."

The Savior
The Bible says that Jesus is the Son of God and equal to the Father in every respect. He's also the son of the virgin Mary. He became human in order to save us. He satisfied the demands of the law in Moses' teachings for everyone by keeping God's commandments for us, and took the punishment we deserved for our sins by suffering and dying in our place on the cross. He came back to life from the dead and lives today. He will return visibly at the world's end to judge everyone (see also Matthew 1:18–25; John 5:18–24; 14:9; Acts 1:11; 10:42; Romans 4:25; Galatians 3:13; 4:4–5; 1 Peter 2:22, 24; 1 John 2:1–2).

---

³¹The Jews had again brought some rocks to stone Jesus to death. ³²Jesus replied to them, "I've shown you many good things that come from the Father.

For which of these good things do you want to stone me to death?"

³³The Jews answered Jesus, "We're going to stone you to death, not for any good things you've done, but for dishonoring God. You claim to be God, although you're only a man."

³⁴Jesus said to them, "Don't your Scriptures say, 'I said, "You are gods"'? ³⁵The Scriptures cannot be discredited. So if God calls people gods (and they are the people to whom he gave the Scriptures), ³⁶why do you say that I'm dishonoring God because I said, 'I'm the Son of God'? God set me apart for this holy purpose and has sent me into the world. ³⁷If I'm not doing the things my Father does, don't believe me. ³⁸But if I'm doing those things and you refuse to believe me, then at least believe the things that I'm doing. Then you will know and recognize that the Father is in me and that I am in the Father."

³⁹The Jews tried to arrest Jesus again, but he got away from them. ⁴⁰He went back across the Jordan River and stayed in the place where John first baptized people.

⁴¹Many people went to Jesus. They said, "John didn't perform any miracles, but everything John said about this man is true." ⁴²Many people there believed in Jesus.

Jesus Brings Lazarus Back to Life

11 ¹Lazarus, who lived in Bethany, the village where Mary and her sister Martha lived, was sick. ²(Mary was the woman who poured perfume on the Lord and wiped his feet with her hair. Her brother Lazarus was the one who was sick.)

³So the sisters sent a messenger to tell Jesus, "Lord, your close friend is sick."

⁴When Jesus heard the message, he said, "His sickness won't result in death. Instead, this sickness will bring glory to God so that the Son of God will receive glory through it."

⁵Jesus loved Martha, her sister, and Lazarus. ⁶Yet, when Jesus heard that Lazarus was sick, he stayed where he was for two more days.

⁷Then, after the two days, Jesus said to his disciples, "Let's go back to Judea."

⁸The disciples said to him, "Rabbi, not long ago the Jews wanted to stone you to death. Do you really want to go back there?"

⁹Jesus answered, "Aren't there twelve hours of daylight? Those who walk during the day don't stumble, because they see the light of this world. ¹⁰However, those who walk at night stumble because they have no light in themselves."

¹¹After Jesus said this, he told his disciples, "Our friend Lazarus is sleeping, and I'm going to Bethany to wake him."

¹²His disciples said to him, "Lord, if he's sleeping, he'll get well."

¹³Jesus meant that Lazarus was dead, but the disciples thought Jesus meant that Lazarus was only sleeping. ¹⁴Then Jesus told them plainly, "Lazarus has died, ¹⁵but I'm glad that I wasn't there so that you can grow in faith. Let's go to Lazarus."

¹⁶Thomas, who was called Didymus, said to the rest of the disciples, "Let's go so that we, too, can die with Jesus."

¹⁷When Jesus arrived, he found that Lazarus had been in the tomb for four days. ¹⁸(Bethany was near Jerusalem, not quite two miles away.) ¹⁹Many Jews had come to Martha and Mary to comfort them about their brother.

²⁰When Martha heard that Jesus was coming, she went to meet him. Mary stayed at home. ²¹Martha told Jesus, "Lord, if you had been here, my brother would not have died. ²²But even now I know that God will give you whatever you ask him."

²³Jesus told Martha, "Your brother will come back to life."

²⁴Martha answered Jesus, "I know that he'll come back to life on the last day, when everyone will come back to life."

²⁵Jesus said to her, "I am the one who brings people back to life, and I am life itself. Those who believe in me will live even if they die. ²⁶Everyone who lives and believes in me will never die. Do you believe that?"

²⁷Martha said to him, "Yes, Lord, I believe that you are the Messiah, the Son of God, the one who was expected to come into the world."

²⁸After Martha had said this, she went back home and whispered to her sister Mary, "The teacher is here, and he is calling for you."

God's Love for Us

When bad things happen, we might question God's love for us. When Mary's brother Lazarus died, she questioned Jesus. Mary thought that if Jesus had been there, Lazarus would still be alive. Jesus, however, knew that God had a greater plan. There may be times when you can't understand what God is doing. But if you trust him, you will eventually see God's greater plan. No matter how difficult your situation may be, trust God. You can trust him to work out things in your life.

---

[29]When Mary heard this, she got up quickly and went to Jesus. [30](Jesus had not yet come into the village but was still where Martha had met him.) [31]The Jews who were comforting Mary in the house saw her get up quickly and leave. So they followed her. They thought that she was going to the tomb to cry. [32]When Mary arrived where Jesus was and saw him, she knelt at his feet and said, "Lord, if you had been here, my brother would not have died."

[33]When Jesus saw her crying, and the Jews who were crying with her, he was deeply moved and troubled.

[34]So Jesus asked, "Where did you put Lazarus?"

They answered him, "Lord, come and see."

[35]Jesus cried. [36]The Jews said, "See how much Jesus loved him." [37]But some of the Jews asked, "Couldn't this man who gave a blind man sight keep Lazarus from dying?"

[38]Deeply moved again, Jesus went to the tomb. It was a cave with a stone covering the entrance. [39]Jesus said, "Take the stone away."

Martha, the dead man's sister, told Jesus, "Lord, there must already be a stench. He's been dead for four days."

[40]Jesus said to her, "Didn't I tell you that if you believe, you would see God's glory?" [41]So the

stone was moved away from the entrance of the tomb.

Jesus looked up and said, "Father, I thank you for hearing me. ⁴²I've known that you always hear me. However, I've said this so that the crowd standing around me will believe that you sent me." ⁴³After Jesus had said this, he shouted as loudly as he could, "Lazarus, come out!"

⁴⁴The dead man came out. Strips of cloth were wound around his feet and hands, and his face was wrapped with a handkerchief. Jesus told them, "Free Lazarus, and let him go."

The Jewish Council Plans to Kill Jesus

⁴⁵Many Jews who had visited Mary and had seen what Jesus had done believed in him. ⁴⁶But some of them went to the Pharisees and told them what Jesus had done. ⁴⁷So the chief priests and the Pharisees called a meeting of the council. They asked, "What are we doing? This man is performing a lot of miracles. ⁴⁸If we let him continue what he's doing, everyone will believe in him. Then the Romans will take away our position and our nation."

⁴⁹One of them, Caiaphas, who was chief priest that year, told them, "You people don't know anything. ⁵⁰You haven't even considered this: It is better for one man to die for the people than for the whole nation to be destroyed."

⁵¹Caiaphas didn't say this on his own. As chief priest that year, he prophesied that Jesus would die for the Jewish nation. ⁵²He prophesied that Jesus wouldn't die merely for this nation, but that

Jesus would die to bring God's scattered children together and make them one.

⁵³From that day on, the Jewish council planned to kill Jesus. ⁵⁴So Jesus no longer walked openly among the Jews. Instead, he left Bethany and went to the countryside near the desert, to a city called Ephraim, where he stayed with his disciples.

⁵⁵The Jewish Passover was near. Many people came from the countryside to Jerusalem to purify themselves before the Passover. ⁵⁶As they stood in the temple courtyard, they looked for Jesus and asked each other, "Do you think that he'll avoid coming to the festival?" ⁵⁷(The chief priests and the Pharisees had given orders that whoever knew where Jesus was should tell them so that they could arrest him.)

Mary Prepares Jesus' Body for the Tomb
(Matthew 26:6–13; Mark 14:3–9)

12 ¹Six days before Passover, Jesus arrived in Bethany. Lazarus, whom Jesus had brought back to life, lived there. ²Dinner was prepared for Jesus in Bethany. Martha served the dinner, and Lazarus was one of the people eating with Jesus.

³Mary took a bottle of very expensive perfume made from pure nard and poured it on Jesus' feet. Then she dried his feet with her hair. The fragrance of the perfume filled the house.

⁴One of his disciples, Judas Iscariot, who was going to betray him, asked, ⁵"Why wasn't this perfume sold for a high price and the money given

to the poor?" ⁶(Judas didn't say this because he cared about the poor but because he was a thief. He was in charge of the moneybag and carried the contributions.) ⁷Jesus said to Judas, "Leave her alone! She has done this to prepare me for the day I will be placed in a tomb. ⁸You will always have the poor with you, but you will not always have me with you."

⁹A large crowd of Jews found out that Jesus was in Bethany. So they went there not only to see Jesus but also to see Lazarus, whom Jesus had brought back to life. ¹⁰The chief priests planned to kill Lazarus too. ¹¹Lazarus was the reason why many people were leaving the Jews and believing in Jesus.

The King Comes to Jerusalem
(Matthew 21:1–11; Mark 11:1–11; Luke 19:29–44)

¹²On the next day the large crowd that had come to the Passover festival heard that Jesus was coming to Jerusalem. ¹³So they took palm branches and went to meet him. They were shouting,

> "Hosanna!
>> Blessed is the one who comes in the name of
>>> the Lord,
>>> the king of Israel!"

¹⁴Jesus obtained a donkey and sat on it, as Scripture says:
>> ¹⁵"Don't be afraid, people of Zion!
>>> Your king is coming.
>>>> He is riding on a donkey's colt."

¹⁶At first Jesus' disciples didn't know what these prophecies meant. However, when Jesus was glorified, the disciples remembered that these prophecies had been written about him. The disciples remembered that they had taken part in fulfilling the prophecies.

¹⁷The people who had been with Jesus when he called Lazarus from the tomb and brought him back to life reported what they had seen. ¹⁸Because the crowd heard that Jesus had performed this miracle, they came to meet him.

¹⁹The Pharisees said to each other, "This is getting us nowhere. Look! The whole world is following him!"

Some Greeks Ask to See Jesus

²⁰Some Greeks were among those who came to worship during the Passover festival. ²¹They went to Philip (who was from Bethsaida in Galilee) and told him, "Sir, we would like to meet Jesus." ²²Philip told Andrew, and they told Jesus.

²³Jesus replied to them, "The time has come for the Son of Man to be glorified. ²⁴I can guarantee this truth: A single grain of wheat doesn't produce anything unless it is planted in the ground and dies. If it dies, it will produce a lot of grain. ²⁵Those who love their lives will destroy them, and those who hate their lives in this world will guard them for everlasting life. ²⁶Those who serve me must follow me. My servants will be with me wherever I will be. If people serve me, the Father will honor them.

²⁷"I am too deeply troubled now to know how to express my feelings. Should I say, 'Father, save me from this time of suffering'? No! I came for this time of suffering. ²⁸Father, give glory to your name."

A voice from heaven said, "I have given it glory, and I will give it glory again."

²⁹The crowd standing there heard the voice and said that it had thundered. Others in the crowd said that an angel had talked to him. ³⁰Jesus replied, "That voice wasn't for my benefit but for yours.

³¹"This world is being judged now. The ruler of this world will be thrown out now. ³²When I have been lifted up from the earth, I will draw all people toward me." ³³By saying this, he indicated how he was going to die.

³⁴The crowd responded to him, "We have heard from the Scriptures that the Messiah will remain here forever. So how can you say, 'The Son of Man must be lifted up from the earth'? Who is this 'Son of Man'?"

³⁵Jesus answered the crowd, "The light will still be with you for a little while. Walk while you have light so that darkness won't defeat you. Those who walk in the dark don't know where they're going. ³⁶While you have the light, believe in the light so that you will become people whose lives show the light."

After Jesus had said this, he was concealed as he left. ³⁷Although they had seen Jesus perform so many miracles, they wouldn't believe in him. ³⁸In this way the words of the prophet Isaiah came true:

"Lord, who has believed our message?
　To whom has the Lord's power been
　　revealed?"

³⁹So the people couldn't believe because, as Isaiah also said,

⁴⁰"God blinded them
　and made them close-minded
　　so that their eyes don't see
　　　and their minds don't understand.
　　And they never turn to me for
　　　healing!"

⁴¹Isaiah said this because he had seen Jesus' glory and had spoken about him. ⁴²Many rulers believed in Jesus. However, they wouldn't admit it publicly because the Pharisees would have thrown them out of the synagogue. ⁴³They were more concerned about what people thought of them than about what God thought of them.

⁴⁴Then Jesus said loudly, "Whoever believes in me believes not only in me but also in the one who sent me. ⁴⁵Whoever sees me sees the one who sent me. ⁴⁶I am the light that has come into the world so that everyone who believes in me will not live in the dark. ⁴⁷If anyone hears my words and doesn't follow them, I don't condemn them. I didn't come to condemn the world but to save the world. ⁴⁸Those who reject me by not accepting what I say have a judge appointed for them. The words that I have spoken will judge them on the last day. ⁴⁹I have not spoken on my own. Instead,

the Father who sent me told me what I should say and how I should say it. ⁵⁰I know that what he commands is eternal life. Whatever I say is what the Father told me to say."

Jesus Washes the Disciples' Feet

13 ¹Before the Passover festival, Jesus knew that the time had come for him to leave this world and go back to the Father. Jesus loved his own who were in the world, and he loved them to the end.

²While supper was taking place, the devil had already put the idea of betraying Jesus into the mind of Judas, son of Simon Iscariot.

³The Father had put everything in Jesus' control. Jesus knew that. He also knew that he had come from God and was going back to God. ⁴So he got up from the table, removed his outer clothes, took a towel, and tied it around his waist. ⁵Then he poured water into a basin and began to wash the disciples' feet and dry them with the towel that he had tied around his waist.

Caring for Others

Do you see the irony in these verses? Jesus, the King of kings and Lord of lords, washed his servants' feet. The example for us is clear: None of us is better than another, and no one should expect to be served. Rather than expect someone to serve you, look for ways to serve someone else. Imitate Jesus' example.

The Bible teaches that holiness of life and conduct follows conversion. In fact, it's the outcome of faith. As a result, every sincere follower of Jesus must be active in doing good things and serving others. Although such holiness is progressive, perfection will not be attained until a person enters eternal life (see also Romans 7:15–25; 2 Corinthians 7:1; Galatians 5:6, 25; Ephesians 2:10; Philippians 3:12–14; 1 Thessalonians 4:3; 1 Peter 1:15).

[6]When Jesus came to Simon Peter, Peter asked him, "Lord, are you going to wash my feet?"

[7]Jesus answered Peter, "You don't know now what I'm doing. You will understand later."

[8]Peter told Jesus, "You will never wash my feet."

Jesus replied to Peter, "If I don't wash you, you don't belong to me."

[9]Simon Peter said to Jesus, "Lord, don't wash only my feet. Wash my hands and my head too!"

[10]Jesus told Peter, "People who have washed are completely clean. They need to have only their feet washed. All of you, except for one, are clean." [11](Jesus knew who was going to betray him. That's why he said, "All of you, except for one, are clean.")

[12]After Jesus had washed their feet and put on his outer clothes, he took his place at the table again. Then he asked his disciples, "Do you understand what I've done for you? [13]You call me teacher and Lord, and you're right because that's what I am. [14]So if I, your Lord and teacher, have washed your feet, you must wash each other's feet. [15]I've given you an example that you should follow. [16]I can guarantee this truth: Slaves are not superior to their owners, and messengers are not superior to the people who send them. [17]If you understand all of this, you are blessed whenever you follow my example.

[18]"I'm not talking about all of you. I know the people I've chosen to be apostles. However, I've

made my choice so that Scripture will come true. It says, 'The one who eats my bread has turned against me.' ¹⁹I'm telling you now before it happens. Then, when it happens, you will believe that I am the one.

²⁰"I can guarantee this truth: Whoever accepts me accepts the one who sent me."

Jesus Knows Who Will Betray Him
(Matthew 26:21–25; Mark 14:18–21; Luke 22:21–23)

²¹After saying this, Jesus was deeply troubled. He declared, "I can guarantee this truth: One of you is going to betray me!"

²²The disciples began looking at each other and wondering which one of them Jesus meant.

²³One disciple, the one whom Jesus loved, was near him at the table. ²⁴Simon Peter motioned to that disciple and said, "Ask Jesus whom he's talking about!"

²⁵Leaning close to Jesus, that disciple asked, "Lord, who is it?"

²⁶Jesus answered, "He's the one to whom I will give this piece of bread after I've dipped it in the sauce." So Jesus dipped the bread and gave it to Judas, son of Simon Iscariot.

²⁷Then, after Judas took the piece of bread, Satan entered him. So Jesus told him, "Hurry! Do what you have to do." ²⁸No one at the table knew why Jesus said this to him. ²⁹Judas had the moneybag. So some thought that Jesus was telling him to buy what they needed for the festival or to give something to the poor.

³⁰Judas took the piece of bread and immediately went outside. It was night.

³¹When Judas was gone, Jesus said, "The Son of Man is now glorified, and because of him God is glorified. ³²If God is glorified because of the Son of Man, God will glorify the Son of Man because of himself, and he will glorify the Son of Man at once."

Jesus Predicts Peter's Denial
(Matthew 26:31–35; Mark 14:27–31; Luke 22:31–34)

³³Jesus said, "Dear children, I will still be with you for a little while. I'm telling you what I told the Jews. You will look for me, but you can't go where I'm going.

³⁴"I'm giving you a new commandment: Love each other in the same way that I have loved you. ³⁵Everyone will know that you are my disciples because of your love for each other."

Loving God and Others

What do your actions say to others about your faith? During his last supper with his disciples, Jesus urged them to love each other. Our actions demonstrate that we are also disciples of Jesus, our Savior. Would someone know that you're a disciple of Jesus by watching what you do?

The Bible teaches that holiness of life and conduct follows conversion. In fact, it's the outcome of faith. As a result, every sincere follower of Jesus must be active in doing good things and serving others. Although such holiness is progressive, perfection will not be attained until a person enters eternal life (see also Romans 7:15–25; 2 Corinthians 7:1; Galatians 5:6, 25; Ephesians 2:10; Philippians 3:12–14; 1 Thessalonians 4:3; 1 Peter 1:15).

³⁶Simon Peter asked him, "Lord, where are you going?"

Jesus answered him, "You can't follow me now to the place where I'm going. However, you will follow me later."

³⁷Peter said to Jesus, "Lord, why can't I follow you now? I'll give my life for you."

³⁸Jesus replied, "Will you give your life for me? I can guarantee this truth: No rooster will crow until you say three times that you don't know me.

Jesus Promises to Send the Holy Spirit

14 ¹"Don't be troubled. Believe in God, and believe in me. ²My Father's house has many rooms. If that were not true, would I have told you that I'm going to prepare a place for you? ³If I go to prepare a place for you, I will come again. Then I will bring you into my presence so that you will be where I am. ⁴You know the way to the place where I am going."

⁵Thomas said to him, "Lord, we don't know where you're going. So how can we know the way?"

⁶Jesus answered him, "I am the way, the truth, and the life. No one goes to the Father except through me. ⁷If you have known me, you will also know my Father. From now on you know him through me and have seen him in me."

The Resurrection

Many people still ask, "Why do Christians insist that believing in Jesus is the only way to obtain eternal life?" If we woke up tomorrow morning and discovered that Mohammed never really existed, it would not affect Islam. If we discovered that Siddhartha Gautama (the founder of Buddhism) never existed, it would not affect Buddhism. Why? Because these religions are based on the teachings of their founders, not on the founders themselves.

However, if we woke up tomorrow and discovered that Jesus never lived, or if he lived but never came back to life after being crucified and buried, Christianity would collapse. The Christian faith rises or falls on the greatest of all miracles—Jesus' coming back to life from the dead. Therefore, when Jesus boldly claims, "I am the way, the truth, and the life. No one goes to the Father except through me," his followers take his words seriously! The book of Acts reveals, "No one else can save us. Indeed, we can be saved only by the power of the one named Jesus" (Acts 4:12). Jesus is the only one who claimed to be God in human form, to be the promised Savior of the world, and to come back to life after being crucified and buried.

⁸Philip said to Jesus, "Lord, show us the Father, and that will satisfy us."

⁹Jesus replied, "I have been with all of you for a long time. Don't you know me yet, Philip? The person who has seen me has seen the Father. So how can you say, 'Show us the Father'? ¹⁰Don't you believe that I am in the Father and the Father is in me? What I'm telling you doesn't come from me. The Father, who lives in me, does what he wants. ¹¹Believe me when I say that I am in the Father and that the Father is in me. Otherwise, believe me because of the things I do.

The Savior

The Bible says that Jesus is the Son of God and equal to the Father in every respect. He's also the son of the virgin Mary. He became human in order to save us. He satisfied the demands of the law in Moses' teachings for everyone by keeping God's commandments for us, and took the punishment we deserved for our sins by suffering and dying in our place on the cross. He came back to life from the dead and lives today. He will return visibly at the world's end to judge everyone (see also Matthew 1:18–25; John 5:18–24; 10:30; Acts 1:11; 10:42; Romans 4:25; Galatians 3:13; 4:4–5; 1 Peter 2:22, 24; 1 John 2:1–2).

¹²"I can guarantee this truth: Those who believe in me will do the things that I am doing. They will do even greater things because I am going to the Father. ¹³I will do anything you ask the Father in my name so that the Father will be given glory because of the Son. ¹⁴If you ask me to do something, I will do it.

¹⁵"If you love me, you will obey my commandments. ¹⁶I will ask the Father, and he will give you another helper who will be with you forever. ¹⁷That helper is the Spirit of Truth. The world cannot accept him, because it doesn't see or know him. You know him, because he lives with you and will be in you.

¹⁸"I will not leave you all alone. I will come back to you. ¹⁹In a little while the world will no longer see me, but you will see me. You will live because I live. ²⁰On that day you will know that I am in my Father and that you are in me and that I am in you. ²¹Whoever knows and obeys my commandments is the person who loves me. Those who love me will have my Father's love, and I, too, will love them and show myself to them."

²²Judas (not Iscariot) asked Jesus, "Lord, what has happened that you are going to reveal yourself to us and not to the world?"

²³Jesus answered him, "Those who love me will do what I say. My Father will love them, and we will go to them and make our home with them. ²⁴A person who doesn't love me doesn't do what I say. I don't make up what you hear me say. What I say comes from the Father who sent me.

²⁵"I have told you this while I'm still with you. ²⁶However, the helper, the Holy Spirit, whom the

Father will send in my name, will teach you everything. He will remind you of everything that I have ever told you.

²⁷"I'm leaving you peace. I'm giving you my peace. I don't give you the kind of peace that the world gives. So don't be troubled or cowardly. ²⁸You heard me tell you, 'I'm going away, but I'm coming back to you.' If you loved me, you would be glad that I'm going to the Father, because the Father is greater than I am."

The Holy Spirit
Do you want help? Would you like comfort? Are you looking for real peace? Do you need assurance of love or protection? Would you like to remember Jesus' teachings? The Holy Spirit provides all these things and more to those who are Christians—who believe that Jesus is truly God and trust him as their only and real Savior. Jesus told his disciples about the Holy Spirit, who would come to be with each of them and all his followers forever.

---

²⁹"I'm telling you this now before it happens. When it does happen, you will believe. ³⁰The ruler of this world has no power over me. But he's coming, so I won't talk with you much longer. ³¹However, I want the world to know that I love the Father and that I am doing exactly what the Father has commanded me to do. Get up! We have to leave."

Jesus, the True Vine

15 ¹Then Jesus said, "I am the true vine, and my Father takes care of the vineyard. ²He removes every one of my branches that doesn't produce fruit. He also prunes every branch that does produce fruit to make it produce more fruit.

³"You are already clean because of what I have told you. ⁴Live in me, and I will live in you. A branch cannot produce any fruit by itself. It has to stay attached to the vine. In the same way, you cannot produce fruit unless you live in me.

⁵"I am the vine. You are the branches. Those who live in me while I live in them will produce a lot of fruit. But you can't produce anything without me. ⁶Whoever doesn't live in me is thrown away like a branch and dries up. Branches like this are gathered, thrown into a fire, and burned. ⁷If you live in me and what I say lives in you, then ask for anything you want, and it will be yours. ⁸You give glory to my Father when you produce a lot of fruit and therefore show that you are my disciples.

⁹"I have loved you the same way the Father has loved me. So live in my love. ¹⁰If you obey my commandments, you will live in my love. I have obeyed my Father's commandments, and in that way I live in his love. ¹¹I have told you this so that you will be as joyful as I am, and your joy will be complete. ¹²Love each other as I have loved you. This is what I'm commanding you to do. ¹³The greatest love you can show is to give your life for your friends. ¹⁴You are my friends if you obey my commandments. ¹⁵I don't call you servants anymore, because a servant doesn't know what his master is doing. But I've called you friends because I've made known to you everything that I've heard from my Father. ¹⁶You didn't choose me, but I chose you. I have appointed you to go,

to produce fruit that will last, and to ask the Father in my name to give you whatever you ask for. ¹⁷Love each other. This is what I'm commanding you to do.

¹⁸"If the world hates you, realize that it hated me before it hated you. ¹⁹If you had anything in common with the world, the world would love you as one of its own. But you don't have anything in common with the world. I chose you from the world, and that's why the world hates you. ²⁰Remember what I told you: 'A servant isn't greater than his master.' If they persecuted me, they will also persecute you. If they did what I said, they will also do what you say. ²¹Indeed, they will do all this to you because you are committed to me, since they don't know the one who sent me. ²²If I hadn't come and spoken to them, they wouldn't have any sin. But now they have no excuse for their sin. ²³The person who hates me also hates my Father. ²⁴If I hadn't done among them what no one else has done, they wouldn't have any sin. But now they have seen and hated both me and my Father. ²⁵In this way what is written in their Scriptures has come true: 'They hate me for no reason.'

²⁶"The helper whom I will send to you from the Father will come. This helper, the Spirit of Truth who comes from the Father, will declare the truth about me. ²⁷You will declare the truth, too, because you have been with me from the beginning."

The Importance of Telling People about Jesus

When you tell others about how you came to know Jesus, you give your friends one of the strongest arguments for becoming a Christian—a follower of Jesus. You alone are an expert witness on the difference Jesus makes in a person's life. Your friends may question the Bible, but they cannot doubt what happened to you. They may argue about the existence of God, but they cannot explain away your own testimony of his presence in your life. That's why Jesus expects us to tell people about him.

Sadness Will Turn to Joy

16 ¹Jesus continued, "I have said these things to you so that you won't lose your faith. ²You will be thrown out of synagogues. Certainly, the time is coming when people who murder you will think that they are serving God. ³They will do these things to you because they haven't known the Father or me. ⁴But I've told you this so that when it happens you'll remember what I've told you. I didn't tell you this at first, because I was with you.

⁵"Now I'm going to the one who sent me. Yet, none of you asks me where I'm going. ⁶But because I've told you this, you're filled with sadness. ⁷However, I am telling you the truth: It's good for you that I'm going away. If I don't go away, the helper won't come to you. But if I go, I will send him to you. ⁸He will come to convict the world of sin, to show the world what has God's approval, and to convince the world that God judges it. ⁹He will convict the world of sin, because people don't believe in me. ¹⁰He will show the world what has God's approval, because I'm going to the Father and you won't see me anymore. ¹¹He will convince the world that God judges it, because the ruler of this world has been judged.

¹²"I have a lot more to tell you, but that would be too much for you now. ¹³When the Spirit of Truth comes, he will guide you into the full truth. He won't speak on his own. He will speak what he hears and will tell you about things to come. ¹⁴He will give me glory, because he will tell you what I say. ¹⁵Everything the Father says is also what I say. That is why I said, 'He will take what I say and tell it to you.'"

Feelings

As your relationship with Jesus matures, you will begin to notice changes in your feelings and emotions. You will find that your emotions respond more and more to what affects the heart of God. You will be disturbed by sin in the world and in your own life. Your heart will ache over a friend's disinterest in Jesus. But you will also experience joy that will last forever because you know the one true God. These verses describe some of the joys and sorrows that Jesus said were in store for his followers.

---

¹⁶"In a little while you won't see me anymore. Then in a little while you will see me again."

¹⁷Some of his disciples said to each other, "What does he mean? He tells us that in a little while we won't see him. Then he tells us that in a little while we will see him again and that he's going to the Father." ¹⁸So they were asking each other, "What does he mean when he says, 'In a little while'? We don't understand what he's talking about."

¹⁹Jesus knew they wanted to ask him something. So he said to them, "Are you trying to figure out among yourselves what I meant when I said, 'In a little while you won't see me, and in a little while you will see me again'? ²⁰I can guarantee this truth: You will cry because you are sad, but

the world will be happy. You will feel pain, but your pain will turn to happiness. ²¹A woman has pain when her time to give birth comes. But after the child is born, she doesn't remember the pain anymore because she's happy that a child has been brought into the world.

²²"Now you're in a painful situation. But I will see you again. Then you will be happy, and no one will take that happiness away from you. ²³When that day comes, you won't ask me any more questions. I can guarantee this truth: If you ask the Father for anything in my name, he will give it to you. ²⁴So far you haven't asked for anything in my name. Ask and you will receive so that you can be completely happy.

²⁵"I have used examples to illustrate these things. The time is coming when I won't use examples to speak to you. Rather, I will speak to you about the Father in plain words. ²⁶When that day comes, you will ask for what you want in my name. I'm telling you that I won't have to ask the Father for you. ²⁷The Father loves you because you have loved me and have believed that I came from God. ²⁸I left the Father and came into the world. Again, as I've said, I'm going to leave the world and go back to the Father."

²⁹His disciples said, "Now you're talking in plain words and not using examples. ³⁰Now we know that you know everything. You don't need to wait for questions to be asked. Because of this, we believe that you have come from God."

³¹Jesus replied to them, "Now you believe. ³²The time is coming, and is already here, when all of you will be scattered. Each of you will go your

own way and leave me all alone. Yet, I'm not all alone, because the Father is with me. ³³I've told you this so that my peace will be with you. In the world you'll have trouble. But cheer up! I have overcome the world."

Real Peace

Two thousand years ago, Jesus gave his followers something that can be ours today: real peace in a troubled and complex world. Jesus knows how difficult things can be, but he also knows that he's greater than any problem.

Many people still say, "But my life is just fine. Why do I need God?" The answer to this question is found in the definition of what is "just fine." Does "just fine" mean that you live with inner peace, in harmony with your family and co-workers, understanding and fulfilling the purpose for which you were created? Nearly all the people who have honestly answered this question admit that their life is not "just fine." In the third century, a very rebellious man named Augustine hit rock bottom and admitted that his life was hopeless. In his despair he found the answer to his greatest need: Jesus. As he grew old he made a very insightful observation. He said that within each person is a God-shaped vacuum. And, until that vacuum is filled by God's truth, people are spiritually empty. People will never experience the fulfillment and real joy intended by God until they have that vacuum filled.

Jesus Prays for Himself, His Disciples, and His Church

17 ¹After saying this, Jesus looked up to heaven and said, "Father, the time is here. Give your Son glory so that your Son can give you glory. ²After all, you've given him authority over all humanity so that he can give eternal life to all those you gave to him. ³This is eternal life: to know you, the only true God, and Jesus Christ, whom you sent. ⁴On earth I have given you glory by finishing the work you gave me to do. ⁵Now, Father, give me glory in your presence with the glory I had with you before the world existed.

⁶"I made your name known to the people you gave me. They are from this world. They belonged to you, and you gave them to me. They did what you told them. ⁷Now they know that everything you gave me comes from you, ⁸because I gave them the message that you gave me. They have accepted this message, and they know for sure that I came from you. They have believed that you sent me.

⁹"I pray for them. I'm not praying for the world but for those you gave me, because they are yours. ¹⁰Everything I have is yours, and everything you have is mine. I have been given glory by the people you have given me. ¹¹I won't be in the world much longer, but they are in the world, and I'm coming back to you. Holy Father, keep them safe by the power of your name, the name that you gave me, so that their unity may be like ours. ¹²While I was with them, I kept them safe by the power of your name, the name that you gave me. I watched over them, and none of them, except one person, became lost. So Scripture came true.

¹³"But now, Father, I'm coming back to you. I say these things while I'm still in the world so that they will have the same joy that I have. ¹⁴I have given them your message. But the world has hated them because they don't belong to the world any more than I belong to the world. ¹⁵I'm not asking you to take them out of the world but to protect them from the evil one. ¹⁶They don't belong to the world any more than I belong to the world.

¹⁷"Use the truth to make them holy. Your words are truth. ¹⁸I have sent them into the world the same way you sent me into the world. ¹⁹I'm dedicating myself to this holy work I'm doing for them so that they, too, will use the truth to be holy.

Popularity

Like a square peg trying to fit into a round hole, a follower of Jesus attempts the impossible when he or she tries to fit in with the rest of the world. In these verses, Jesus prayed for those who believe in him to realize they will never belong in a group of people who live according to the world's standards. And yet sometimes you may still struggle to feel totally accepted and understood by friends and family members who are not Christians. The world will never fully accept you because of the difference Jesus has made in you. Rather than feel depressed that you don't fit in, be glad that you belong instead to Jesus.

²⁰"I'm not praying only for them. I'm also praying for those who will believe in me through their message. ²¹I pray that all of these people continue to have unity in the way that you, Father, are in me and I am in you. I pray that they may be united with us so that the world will believe that you have sent me. ²²I have given them the glory that you gave me. I did this so that they are united in the same way we are. ²³I am in them, and you are in me. So they are completely united. In this way the world knows that you have sent me and that you have loved them in the same way you have loved me.

²⁴"Father, I want those you have given to me to be with me, to be where I am. I want them to see my glory, which you gave me because you loved me before the world was made. ²⁵Righ-

teous Father, the world didn't know you. Yet, I knew you, and these disciples have known that you sent me. ²⁶I have made your name known to them, and I will make it known so that the love you have for me will be in them and I will be in them."

Jesus Is Arrested
(Matthew 26:47–56; Mark 14:43–52; Luke 22:47–54)

18 ¹After Jesus finished his prayer, he went with his disciples to the other side of the Kidron Valley. They entered the garden that was there.

²Judas, who betrayed him, knew the place because Jesus and his disciples often gathered there. ³So Judas took a troop of soldiers and the guards from the chief priests and Pharisees and went to the garden. They were carrying lanterns, torches, and weapons.

⁴Jesus knew everything that was going to happen to him. So he went to meet them and asked, "Who are you looking for?"

⁵They answered him, "Jesus from Nazareth."

Jesus told them, "I am he."

Judas, who betrayed him, was standing with the crowd. ⁶When Jesus told them, "I am he," the crowd backed away and fell to the ground.

⁷Jesus asked them again, "Who are you looking for?"

They said, "Jesus from Nazareth."

⁸Jesus replied, "I told you that I am he. So if you are looking for me, let these other men go."

⁹In this way what Jesus had said came true: "I lost none of those you gave me."

¹⁰Simon Peter had a sword. He drew it, attacked the chief priest's servant, and cut off the servant's right ear. (The servant's name was Malchus.)

¹¹Jesus told Peter, "Put your sword away. Shouldn't I drink the cup of suffering that my Father has given me?"

¹²Then the army officer and the Jewish guards arrested Jesus. They tied Jesus up ¹³and took him first to Annas, the father-in-law of Caiaphas. Caiaphas, the chief priest that year, ¹⁴was the person who had advised the Jews that it was better to have one man die for the people.

Peter Denies Jesus
(Matthew 26:69–75; Mark 14:66–72; Luke 22:54–62)

¹⁵Simon Peter and another disciple followed Jesus. The other disciple was well-known to the chief priest. So that disciple went with Jesus into the chief priest's courtyard. ¹⁶Peter, however, was standing outside the gate. The other disciple talked to the woman who was the gatekeeper and brought Peter into the courtyard.

¹⁷The gatekeeper asked Peter, "Aren't you one of this man's disciples too?"

Peter answered, "No, I'm not!"

¹⁸The servants and the guards were standing around a fire they had built and were warming themselves because it was cold. Peter was standing there, too, and warming himself with the others.

The Chief Priest Questions Jesus

¹⁹The chief priest questioned Jesus about his disciples and his teachings.

²⁰Jesus answered him, "I have spoken publicly for everyone to hear. I have always taught in synagogues or in the temple courtyard, where all the Jews gather. I haven't said anything in secret. ²¹Why do you question me? Question those who heard what I said to them. They know what I've said."

²²When Jesus said this, one of the guards standing near Jesus slapped his face and said, "Is that how you answer the chief priest?"

²³Jesus replied to him, "If I've said anything wrong, tell me what it was. But if I've told the truth, why do you hit me?"

²⁴Annas sent Jesus to Caiaphas, the chief priest. Jesus was still tied up.

Peter Denies Jesus Again
(Matthew 26:69–75; Mark 14:66–72; Luke 22:54–62)

²⁵Simon Peter continued to stand and warm himself by the fire. Some men asked him, "Aren't you, too, one of his disciples?"

Peter denied it by saying, "No, I'm not!"

²⁶One of the chief priest's servants, a relative of the man whose ear Peter had cut off, asked him, "Didn't I see you with Jesus in the garden?"

²⁷Peter again denied it, and just then a rooster crowed.

Pilate Questions Jesus

(Matthew 27:11–14; Mark 15:1–5; Luke 23:1–4)

²⁸Early in the morning, Jesus was taken from Caiaphas' house to the governor's palace.

The Jews wouldn't go into the palace. They didn't want to become unclean, since they wanted to eat the Passover. ²⁹So Pilate came out to them and asked, "What accusation are you making against this man?"

³⁰The Jews answered Pilate, "If he weren't a criminal, we wouldn't have handed him over to you."

³¹Pilate told the Jews, "Take him, and try him by your law."

The Jews answered him, "We're not allowed to execute anyone." ³²In this way what Jesus had predicted about how he would die came true.

³³Pilate went back into the palace, called for Jesus, and asked him, "Are you the king of the Jews?"

³⁴Jesus replied, "Did you think of that yourself, or did others tell you about me?"

³⁵Pilate answered, "Am I a Jew? Your own people and the chief priests handed you over to me. What have you done?"

³⁶Jesus answered, "My kingdom doesn't belong to this world. If my kingdom belonged to this world, my followers would fight to keep me from being handed over to the Jews. My kingdom doesn't have its origin on earth."

The Church—The Community of Believers
The Bible reveals that there is an *invisible* church that consists of all who truly accept Jesus as their real and only Savior. This church is one, Jesus is

its only head and Lord, and all members thereof enjoy equal rights. This church may be found wherever the Good News of Jesus is known. This church will endure forever.

The Bible also teaches that there is a *visible* church, consisting of everyone who professes the Christian faith and gathers about God's word. Sad to say, because of corrupt human nature, there will always be hypocrites and defenders of false teachings and unchristian practices in the church. Therefore, it's the duty of every sincere Christian to search for and unite with that part of the *visible* church that stands for the pure preaching and right practice of God's word (see also Isaiah 55:10–11; Matthew 13:47–48; 15:9; 16:18; 22:2–14; Luke 17:20–21; John 8:31–32; Romans 16:17; 1 Corinthians 11:18; 12:13; 2 Corinthians 6:14–18; Ephesians 1:22–23; 2:19–22; 2 Thessalonians 3:6, 14).

---

³⁷Pilate asked him, "So you are a king?" Jesus replied, "You're correct in saying that I'm a king. I have been born and have come into the world for this reason: to testify to the truth. Everyone who belongs to the truth listens to me."

³⁸Pilate said to him, "What is truth?"

After Pilate said this, he went out to the Jews again and told them, "I don't find this man guilty of anything. ³⁹You have a custom that I should free one person for you at Passover. Would you like me to free the king of the Jews for you?"

⁴⁰The Jews shouted again, "Don't free this man! Free Barabbas!" (Barabbas was a political revolutionary.)

The Soldiers Make Fun of Jesus
(Matthew 27:27–30; Mark 15:16–19)

19 ¹Then Pilate had Jesus taken away and whipped. ²The soldiers twisted some thorny branches into a crown, placed it on his head, and put a purple cape on him. ³They went up to him, said, "Long live the king of the Jews!" and slapped his face.

The People Want Jesus Crucified

⁴Pilate went outside again and told the Jews, "I'm bringing him out to you to let you know that I don't find this man guilty of anything." ⁵Jesus went outside. He was wearing the crown of thorns and the purple cape. Pilate said to the Jews, "Look, here's the man!"

⁶When the chief priests and the guards saw Jesus, they shouted, "Crucify him! Crucify him!"

Pilate told them, "You take him and crucify him. I don't find this man guilty of anything."

⁷The Jews answered Pilate, "We have a law, and by that law he must die because he claimed to be the Son of God."

⁸When Pilate heard them say that, he became more afraid than ever. ⁹He went into the palace again and asked Jesus, "Where are you from?" But Jesus didn't answer him.

¹⁰So Pilate said to Jesus, "Aren't you going to answer me? Don't you know that I have the authority to free you or to crucify you?"

¹¹Jesus answered Pilate, "You wouldn't have any authority over me if it hadn't been given to you from above. That's why the man who handed me over to you is guilty of a greater sin."

¹²When Pilate heard what Jesus said, he wanted to free him. But the Jews shouted, "If you free this man, you're not a friend of the emperor. Anyone who claims to be a king is defying the emperor."

¹³When Pilate heard what they said, he took Jesus outside and sat on the judge's seat in a place called Stone Pavement. (In Hebrew it is called *Gabbatha*.) ¹⁴The time was about six o'clock in the morning on the Friday of the Passover festival.

Pilate said to the Jews, "Look, here's your king!"

¹⁵Then the Jews shouted, "Kill him! Kill him! Crucify him!"

Pilate asked them, "Should I crucify your king?"

The chief priests responded, "The emperor is the only king we have!"

¹⁶Then Pilate handed Jesus over to them to be crucified.

The Crucifixion
(Matthew 27:31–44; Mark 15:20–32; Luke 23:26–38)

So the soldiers took Jesus. ¹⁷He carried his own cross and went out of the city to a location called The Skull. (In Hebrew this place is called *Golgotha*.) ¹⁸The soldiers crucified Jesus and two other men there. Jesus was in the middle.

¹⁹Pilate wrote a notice and put it on the cross. The notice read, "Jesus from Nazareth, the king of the Jews." ²⁰Many Jews read this notice, because the place where Jesus was crucified was near the city. The notice was written in Hebrew, Latin, and Greek.

²¹The chief priests of the Jewish people told Pilate, "Don't write, 'The king of the Jews!' Instead, write, 'He said that he is the king of the Jews.'"

²²Pilate replied, "I have written what I've written."

²³When the soldiers had crucified Jesus, they took his clothes and divided them four ways so that each soldier could have a share. His robe was left over. It didn't have a seam because it had been woven in one piece from top to bottom. ²⁴The soldiers said to each other, "Let's not rip it apart. Let's throw dice to see who will get it." In this way the Scripture came true: "They divided my clothes among themselves. They threw dice for my clothing." So that's what the soldiers did.

²⁵Jesus' mother, her sister, Mary (the wife of Clopas), and Mary from Magdala were standing beside Jesus' cross. ²⁶Jesus saw his mother and the disciple whom he loved standing there. He said to his mother, "Look, here's your son!" ²⁷Then he said to the disciple, "Look, here's your mother!"

From that time on she lived with that disciple in his home.

Family

Can you imagine what Mary felt standing at the foot of her son's cross? Seeing Jesus in pain, agony, and humiliation must have devastated her. While on the cross, Jesus asked John to take care of his mother. Jesus knew that his mother would need special care and attention in the days to come. How do you feel when you see family members in pain? These verses speak about Jesus' example.

Jesus Dies on the Cross
(Matthew 27:45–56; Mark 15:33–41; Luke 23:44–49)

²⁸After this, when Jesus knew that everything had now been finished, he said, "I'm thirsty."

He said this so that Scripture could finally be concluded.

²⁹A jar filled with vinegar was there. So the soldiers put a sponge soaked in the vinegar on a hyssop stick and held it to his mouth.

³⁰After Jesus had taken the vinegar, he said, "It is finished!"

Then he bowed his head and died.

³¹Since it was Friday and the next day was an especially important day of worship, the Jews didn't want the bodies to stay on the crosses. So they asked Pilate to have the men's legs broken and their bodies removed. ³²The soldiers broke the legs of the first man and then of the other man who had been crucified with Jesus.

³³When the soldiers came to Jesus and saw that he was already dead, they didn't break his legs. ³⁴However, one of the soldiers stabbed Jesus' side with his spear, and blood and water immediately came out. ³⁵The one who saw this is an eyewitness. What he says is true, and he knows that he is telling the truth so that you, too, will believe.

³⁶This happened so that the Scripture would come true: "None of his bones will be broken." ³⁷Another Scripture passage says, "They will look at the person whom they have stabbed."

Jesus Is Buried
(Matthew 27:57–61; Mark 15:42–47; Luke 23:50–56)

³⁸Later Joseph from the city of Arimathea asked Pilate to let him remove Jesus' body. (Joseph was a disciple of Jesus but secretly because he was

afraid of the Jews). Pilate gave him permission to remove Jesus' body. So Joseph removed it. ³⁹Nicodemus, the one who had first come to Jesus at night, went with Joseph and brought 75 pounds of a myrrh and aloe mixture.

⁴⁰These two men took the body of Jesus and bound it with strips of linen. They laced the strips with spices. This was the Jewish custom for burial.

⁴¹A garden was located in the place where Jesus was crucified. In that garden was a new tomb in which no one had yet been placed. ⁴²Joseph and Nicodemus put Jesus in that tomb, since that day was the Jewish day of preparation and since the tomb was nearby.

Jesus Comes Back to Life
(Matthew 28:1–10; Mark 16:1–8; Luke 24:1–12)

20 ¹Early on Sunday morning, while it was still dark, Mary from Magdala went to the tomb. She saw that the stone had been removed from the tomb's entrance. ²So she ran to Simon Peter and the other disciple, whom Jesus loved. She told them, "They have removed the Lord from the tomb, and we don't know where they've put him."

³So Peter and the other disciple headed for the tomb. ⁴The two were running side by side, but the other disciple ran faster than Peter and came to the tomb first. ⁵He bent over and looked inside the tomb. He saw the strips of linen lying there but didn't go inside.

⁶Simon Peter arrived after him and went into the tomb. He saw the strips of linen lying there. ⁷He also saw the cloth that had been on Jesus' head. It wasn't lying with the strips of linen but was rolled up separately. ⁸Then the other disciple, who arrived at the tomb first, went inside. He saw and believed. ⁹They didn't know yet what Scripture meant when it said that Jesus had to come back to life. ¹⁰So the disciples went back home.

Jesus Appears to Mary from Magdala

¹¹Mary, however, stood there and cried as she looked at the tomb. As she cried, she bent over and looked inside. ¹²She saw two angels in white clothes. They were sitting where the body of Jesus had been lying. One angel was where Jesus' head had been, and the other was where his feet had been. ¹³The angels asked her why she was crying.

Mary told them, "They have removed my Lord, and I don't know where they've put him."

¹⁴After she said this, she turned around and saw Jesus standing there. However, she didn't know that it was Jesus. ¹⁵Jesus asked her, "Why are you crying? Who are you looking for?"

Mary thought it was the gardener speaking to her. So she said to him, "Sir, if you carried him away, tell me where you have put him, and I'll remove him."

¹⁶Jesus said to her, "Mary!"

Mary turned around and said to him in Hebrew, "Rabboni!" (This word means "teacher.")

¹⁷Jesus told her, "Don't hold on to me. I have not yet gone to the Father. But go to my brothers and sisters and tell them, 'I am going to my Father and your Father, to my God and your God.'"

¹⁸Mary from Magdala went to the disciples and told them, "I have seen the Lord." She also told them what he had said to her.

Jesus Appears to the Disciples
(Luke 24:36–48)

¹⁹That Sunday evening, the disciples were together behind locked doors because they were afraid of the Jews. Jesus stood among them and said to them, "Peace be with you!" ²⁰When he said this, he showed them his hands and his side. The disciples were glad to see the Lord.

²¹Jesus said to them again, "Peace be with you! As the Father has sent me, so I am sending you." ²²After he had said this, he breathed on the disciples and said, "Receive the Holy Spirit. ²³Whenever you forgive sins, they are forgiven. Whenever you don't forgive them, they are not forgiven."

Jesus Appears to Thomas

²⁴Thomas, one of the twelve apostles, who was called Didymus, wasn't with them when Jesus came. ²⁵The other disciples told him, "We've seen the Lord."

Thomas told them, "I refuse to believe this unless I see the nail marks in his hands, put my fingers into them, and put my hand into his side."

²⁶A week later Jesus' disciples were again in the house, and Thomas was with them. Even though the doors were locked, Jesus stood among them and said, "Peace be with you!" ²⁷Then Jesus said to Thomas, "Put your finger here, and look at my hands. Take your hand, and put it into my side. Stop doubting, and believe."

²⁸Thomas responded to Jesus, "My Lord and my God!"

²⁹Jesus said to Thomas, "You believe because you've seen me. Blessed are those who haven't seen me but believe."

Doubt

Thomas, the apostle who doubted, wasn't punished for his reluctance to accept the fact that Jesus came back to life after being crucified. Instead, Jesus gently allowed him to see the truth for himself. But what an exciting promise Jesus extends to those of us who weren't privileged to walk and talk with him. We will be especially rewarded for believing without seeing. That's a great reminder when doubts arise!

---

³⁰Jesus performed many other miracles that his disciples saw. Those miracles are not written in this book. ³¹But these miracles have been written so that you will believe that Jesus is the Messiah, the Son of God, and so that you will have life by believing in him.

Jesus Appears to His Disciples Again

21 ¹Later, by the Sea of Tiberias, Jesus showed himself again to the disciples. This is what happened. ²Simon Peter, Thomas (called Didymus), Nathanael from Cana in Galilee, Zebedee's sons, and two other disciples of Jesus were together. ³Simon Peter said to the others, "I'm going fishing."

They told him, "We're going with you."

They went out in a boat but didn't catch a thing that night. ⁴As the sun was rising, Jesus stood on the shore. The disciples didn't realize that it was Jesus.

⁵Jesus asked them, "Friends, haven't you caught any fish?"

They answered him, "No, we haven't."

⁶He told them, "Throw the net out on the right side of the boat, and you'll catch some." So they threw the net out and were unable to pull it in because so many fish were in it.

⁷The disciple whom Jesus loved said to Peter, "It's the Lord." When Simon Peter heard that it was the Lord, he put back on the clothes that he had taken off and jumped into the sea. ⁸The other disciples came with the boat and dragged the net full of fish. They weren't far from the shore, only about 100 yards.

⁹When they went ashore, they saw a fire with a fish lying on the coals, and they saw a loaf of bread.

¹⁰Jesus told them, "Bring some of the fish you've just caught." Simon Peter got into the boat and pulled the net ashore. Though the net was filled with 153 large fish, it was not torn.

¹²Jesus told them, "Come, have breakfast." None of the disciples dared to ask him who he was. They

knew he was the Lord. ¹³Jesus took the bread, gave it to them, and did the same with the fish.

¹⁴This was the third time that Jesus showed himself to the disciples after he had come back to life.

Jesus Speaks with Peter

¹⁵After they had eaten breakfast, Jesus asked Simon Peter, "Simon, son of John, do you love me more than the other disciples do?"

Peter answered him, "Yes, Lord, you know that I love you."

Jesus told him, "Feed my lambs."

¹⁶Jesus asked him again, a second time, "Simon, son of John, do you love me?"

Peter answered him, "Yes, Lord, you know that I love you."

Jesus told him, "Take care of my sheep."

¹⁷Jesus asked him a third time, "Simon, son of John, do you love me?"

Peter felt sad because Jesus had asked him a third time, "Do you love me?" So Peter said to him, "Lord, you know everything. You know that I love you."

Jesus told him, "Feed my sheep. ¹⁸I can guarantee this truth: When you were young, you would get ready to go where you wanted. But when you're old, you will stretch out your hands, and someone else will get you ready to take you where you don't want to go." ¹⁹Jesus said this to show by what kind of death Peter would bring glory to God. After saying this, Jesus told Peter, "Follow me!"

²⁰Peter turned around and saw the disciple whom Jesus loved. That disciple was following them. He was the one who leaned against Jesus' chest at the supper and asked, "Lord, who is going to betray you?" ²¹When Peter saw him, he asked Jesus, "Lord, what about him?"

²²Jesus said to Peter, "If I want him to live until I come again, how does that concern you? Follow me!" ²³So a rumor that that disciple wouldn't die spread among Jesus' followers. But Jesus didn't say that he wouldn't die. What Jesus said was, "If I want him to live until I come again, how does that concern you?"

²⁴This disciple was an eyewitness of these things and wrote them down. We know that what he says is true.

²⁵Jesus also did many other things. If every one of them were written down, I suppose the world wouldn't have enough room for the books that would be written.

4

The Basics of Faith

The Apostles' Creed

You can also express your faith using the words of the Apostles' Creed:

I believe in God, the almighty Father, the maker of heaven and earth.

I believe in Jesus Christ, God's only Son, our Lord. He was conceived by the Holy Spirit and the Virgin Mary gave birth to him. He suffered at the hands of Pontius Pilate, was crucified, died and was buried. He went down into hell. He came back to life three days after he died. He went up into heaven and took the highest position of power with God, the almighty Father. He will come back from heaven to judge the living and the dead.

I believe in the Holy Spirit, the holy Christian church,

the unity of believers, the forgiveness of sins, the body coming back to life, and living forever. Amen.

A creed, as the word itself implies (Latin: *credo*—"I believe"), is simply a statement of what one believes. Every sincere follower of Jesus has a creed, whether he or she admits it or not. A true creed is not an addition to the Bible, but only an emphasis of the truth of the Bible (see Matthew 10:32; 1 Peter 3:15). Although the Apostles' Creed is not part of the Bible, it is an accurate summary of the teachings of the Christian church. The statements in this expression of faith date back to the first centuries of the church.

The First Article

The first article of the Creed is about God creating us: "I believe in God, the almighty Father, the maker of heaven and earth." What does this mean?

I believe that God has made me and every creature.

He has given me my body and soul, eyes, ears, all the other parts of my body, my mind, and all my senses.

He continues to take care of everything he has given me.

He also gives me clothing and shoes, food and drink, house and home, spouse and children, property, animals, and everything I have.

Every day he richly provides me with everything I need to live.

God defends me from danger.

He guards and protects me from evil.

He does all of these things because of his fatherly, divine goodness and mercy.

I have done nothing to earn this, and I do not deserve this.

Therefore, it is my duty to thank, praise, serve, and obey him.

This is most certainly true!

The Second Article

The second article of the Creed is about God reclaiming us:

I believe in Jesus Christ, God's only Son, our Lord. He was conceived by the Holy Spirit and the virgin Mary gave birth to him. He suffered at the hands of Pontius Pilate, was crucified, died and was placed in a tomb. He went down into hell. He came back to life three days after he died. He went up into heaven and took the highest position of power with God, the almighty Father. He will come back from heaven to judge the living and the dead.

What does this mean?

I believe that Jesus Christ is really God, the only Son of the Father from eternity, and really human, the son of the virgin Mary.

Jesus Christ is my Lord.

He has reclaimed me because I was a lost and condemned creature.

He has set me free from all sins, from death, and from the power of the devil.

He did not use gold or silver to gain my release, but he used his holy, precious blood, and his innocent suffering and death.

He did this so I would be his own and serve him in his kingdom.

Since he has declared me innocent and I have his approval and blessing, I can serve him forever.

He came back from the dead, and he lives and rules throughout all eternity.

This is most certainly true!

The Third Article

The third article of the Creed is about God making us holy. "I believe in the Holy Spirit, the holy Christian church, the unity of believers, the forgiveness of sins, the body coming back to life, and living forever. Amen." What does this mean?

I believe that I cannot bring myself to believe in Jesus Christ, my Lord, through my own intellectual and physical powers.

The Holy Spirit has called me by the Good News, used his gifts to reveal the truth to me, made me holy, and kept me in the true faith.

The Holy Spirit also calls, gathers, and reveals the truth to the whole Christian church on earth.

He makes the whole Christian church on earth holy and

keeps it united with Jesus Christ in the one true faith.

Through the Christian church he richly forgives all my sins and the sins of all believers every day.

On the last day he will bring me and all who have died back to life, and he will give me and all who believe in Christ eternal life.

This is most certainly true!

5

What Does God
Want You to Do?

So, now what? What does God want Christians to do?

First, God Wants You to Worship Him

> Give to the LORD the glory his name deserves.
>   Worship the LORD in his holy splendor.
>
> Psalm 29:2

> Come, let's worship and bow down.
>   Let's kneel in front of the LORD, our maker,
>   because he is our God
>   and we are the people in his care,
>   the flock that he leads.
>
> Psalm 95:6–7

Worship and glory belong forever to the eternal king, the immortal, invisible, and only God. Amen.

1 Timothy 1:17

We must also consider how to encourage each other to show love and to do good things. We should not stop gathering together with other believers, as some of you are doing. Instead, we must continue to encourage each other even more as we see the day of the Lord coming.

Hebrews 10:24–25

Second, God Wants You to Spread This Good News

You are chosen people, a royal priesthood, a holy nation, people who belong to God. You were chosen to tell about the excellent qualities of God, who called you out of darkness into his marvelous light. Once you were not God's people, but now you are.

1 Peter 2:9–10

Third, God Wants You to Serve Others

Brothers and sisters, in view of all we have just shared about God's compassion toward us, I encourage you to offer your bodies as living sacrifices, dedicated to God and pleasing to him. . . . Then you will always be able to determine what God really wants—what is good, pleasing, and perfect.

Romans 12:1–2

God has made us what we are. He has created us in Christ
Jesus to live lives filled with good works that he has prepared for us to do.

Ephesians 2:10

He also gave apostles, prophets, missionaries, as well as
pastors and teachers as gifts to his church. Their purpose
is to prepare God's people to serve, and to build up the
body of Christ.

Ephesians 4:11–12

What you do to serve others not only provides for the
needs of God's people, but also produces more and more
prayers of thanksgiving to God. You will honor God through
this genuine act of service because of your commitment
to spread the Good News of Christ and because of your
generosity in sharing with them and everyone else.

2 Corinthians 9:12–13

6

How to Pray

The Lord's Prayer

Prayer and God's word are inseparable—they go together. In and through his word, God speaks to you. In and through prayer, you speak to God.

When you pray, go to your room and close the door. Pray privately to your Father who is with you. Your Father sees what you do in private. He will reward you.

When you pray, don't ramble like heathens who think they'll be heard if they talk a lot. Don't be like them. Your Father knows what you need before you ask him.

This is how you should pray:

Our Father in heaven,
let your name be kept holy.

Let your kingdom come.
Let your will be done on earth
as it is done in heaven.
Give us our daily bread today.
Forgive us as we forgive others.
Don't allow us to be tempted.
Instead, rescue us from the evil one.

Matthew 6:6–13

The Lord's Prayer

Introduction

"Our father in heaven." What does this mean? God uses these words to lovingly invite us to believe that he is our true Father and that we are his true children. He invites us with these words so that we will cheerfully and confidently pray to him in the same way children would ask their dear father for something.

The First Request

"Let your name be kept holy." What does this mean? God's name is holy all by itself. However, we pray in this request that his name will become holy in our lives.

How is that done? God's name becomes holy when people teach the Bible in its truth and purity, and when we, as God's children, make our lives conform to its teachings. Help us to do this, dear Father in heaven! However, anyone who teaches or lives in a way that is different from what the Bible teaches abuses God's name among us. Heavenly Father, prevent this from happening!

The Second Request

"Let your kingdom come." What does this mean? God's kingdom comes all by itself, without our prayers. However, we pray in this request that his kingdom will come to us.

How is that done? God's kingdom comes when our heavenly Father gives us his Holy Spirit. He gives us the Holy Spirit through his words in the Bible. Through his gifts we can believe in God and lead a godly life not only here in the present, but also in the life to come.

The Third Request

"Let your will be done on earth as it is in heaven." What does this mean? God carries out his good and merciful will all by himself, without our prayers. However, we pray in this request that God would carry out his will through us as his willing servants.

How is that done? God's will is carried out when he neutralizes and blocks every evil plan or desire that would like to prevent us from making God's name holy or letting his kingdom come, such as the will of the devil, the world, and our bodies. God's good and merciful will is also carried out when he strengthens and keeps us firm through his Word and our faith to the end.

The Fourth Request

"Give us our daily bread today." What does this mean? God gives daily bread without our prayers, even to all the wicked people. However, we pray in this request that God would lead us to recognize that he is the source of our daily bread and to be grateful when we accept it.

What is meant by daily bread? Daily bread refers to everything that supplies what our bodies need, such as food, drink, clothes, shoes, a home, fields, cattle, money, goods, an honest spouse, honest children, honest workers, honest and faithful rulers, a good government, good weather, peace, good health, a good education, a good reputation, good friends, dependable neighbors, and other similar blessings.

The Fifth Request

"Forgive us as we forgive others." What does this mean? We pray in this request that our Father in heaven would not take our sins into account, or refuse to answer our prayers because of them. We do not deserve the things for which we pray, nor have we earned them. Nevertheless, we ask that he would give us what we pray for because of his kindness. We sin a lot every day and deserve nothing but punishment. That is why we forgive those who sin against us, without any hesitation, and stand ready to help them.

The Sixth Request

"Don't allow us to be tempted." What does this mean? God doesn't tempt anyone. However, we pray in this request that God would guard and keep us, so that the devil, the world, and our own bodies cannot deceive us or lead us into false teachings, despair, or other terrible and shameful sins. We also pray that we will overcome the temptations that try to wear us down, and in the end will be victorious.

The Seventh Request

"Instead, rescue us from the evil one." What does this mean? We sum everything up when we pray in this request that our Father in heaven would rescue us from every evil, whether it affects our bodies, souls, property, or honor. We also pray that when our last hour comes, our Father will grant us a blessed end to our life. Finally, we pray that he will kindly take us from this world of misery to himself in heaven.

Amen

What is meant by the word "Amen"? Amen means that we should be certain that the requests in this prayer are acceptable to our Father in heaven, and are heard by him. The Father not only commanded us to pray in this manner, but he has also promised to hear us. Amen means "Yes, it will certainly happen."

From one end of the Bible to the other there's a record of those whose prayers have been answered. Renew your strength and your relationship with the one true God each day by reading his life-changing Word and by praying according to his will. The following passages will provide you with guidance and real hope.

> That's why I tell you to have faith that you have already received whatever you pray for, and it will be yours. Whenever you pray, forgive anything you have against anyone. Then your Father in heaven will forgive your failures.

Mark 11:24–25

If you live in me and what I say lives in you, then ask for anything you want, and it will be yours.

John 15:7

I can guarantee this truth: If you ask the Father for anything in my name, he will give it to you. So far you haven't asked for anything in my name. Ask and you will receive so that you can be completely happy.

John 16:23–24

Be happy in your confidence, be patient in trouble, and pray continually.

Romans 12:12

If any of you are having trouble, pray.

James 5:13

Dear friends, use your most holy faith to grow. Pray with the Holy Spirit's help.

Jude 1:20

Prayers offered by those who have God's approval are effective.

James 5:16

7

A Quick Guide
to Passages of Hope

The Holy Bible in Clear, Natural English

"GOD'S WORD® is an easy-to-understand Bible translation....It is a wonderful version."
~ REV. BILLY GRAHAM

GOD'S WORD Translation (GW) accurately translates the meaning of the original texts into clear, everyday language. Readable and reliable, GW is living, active, and life-changing.

THE COMBINATION OF ACCURACY AND READABILITY MAKES GW IDEALLY SUITED FOR THE FOLLOWING:

- Devotional reading and in-depth study
- Preaching, teaching, and worship
- Memorization
- Discipleship
- Outreach and evangelism

Find out more at www.GODSWORDTranslation.org.